Dream Interpretation Decoded

Explore Science, Spirituality & Cultural Influences When Understanding Signs and Symbols in Your Dreams

Victor Nyx

Contents

Introduction

Every night as we close our eyes, we embark on mysterious journeys through landscapes of our own creation. Dreams sweep us into worlds where physics holds no power, where past and present blend, and where the impossible becomes our temporary reality. These nightly adventures aren't mere entertainment - they're windows into our deepest thoughts, fears, hopes, and desires.

The human mind processes countless experiences, emotions, and thoughts throughout each day. While our conscious mind might forget or filter many of these, our subconscious carefully stores them away. During sleep, these hidden fragments emerge, weaving themselves into the intricate tapestries we call dreams.

Think of your subconscious mind as a vast ocean. On the surface, you see the waves of your daily thoughts and actions. But beneath lies an entire ecosystem of memories, unprocessed emotions, and deep-seated beliefs. Dreams act as submarines, allowing us brief glimpses into these depths.

Neuroscience suggests dreams play crucial roles in memory consolidation and emotional processing. When we dream, our brains sort through daily experiences, strengthening important memories while discarding unnecessary details. This process helps us learn from experiences and adapt to life's challenges.

Yet dreams hold significance beyond their biological function. Many cultures throughout history have viewed dreams as gateways to spiritual wisdom. These spiritual perspectives suggest dreams connect us to something larger than ourselves. They can provide guidance, warnings, or insights that our conscious minds might miss. A dream about a deceased loved one might bring comfort or closure. A recurring symbol might point toward an important life decision.

Rather than viewing these scientific and spiritual perspectives as contradictory, consider them complementary ways of understanding the same phenomenon. Just as light can be described as both a wave and a particle, dreams can be understood through multiple frameworks. The biological mechanisms that create dreams don't diminish their potential spiritual significance, and spiritual interpretations don't contradict scientific findings.

As you begin this journey of dream exploration, remember that your subconscious speaks a unique language - one shaped by your personal experiences, cultural background, and individual perspectives. What a symbol means to someone else might hold an entirely different significance for you.

1

The Neuroscience of REM Sleep

E very night, as you drift off to sleep, your brain embarks on a fascinating journey through different sleep stages. While dreams can occur in any stage, it's during REM sleep that our most vivid and memorable dreams unfold. But what exactly happens in your brain during this remarkable state?

Think of your brain as a complex theater. During REM sleep, different regions take on specific roles in creating your dream experience. At the base of your brain sits a small but mighty structure called the pontine tegmentum - the director of this nightly performance. When activated, it sends signals that trigger the REM state, much like a director calling "action" on a movie set.

As REM sleep begins, your brain chemistry shifts dramatically. Certain neurotransmitters - the chemical messengers in your brain - change their activity patterns. Norepinephrine and serotonin, which keep you alert during the day, decrease significantly. Meanwhile, acetylcholine levels increase - chemical messengers that plays a crucial role in the nervous system - promoting the vivid mental activity that characterizes your dreams.

"But why does my body feel paralyzed during these vivid dreams?" This natural phenomenon, called REM atonia, happens when your brain temporarily disconnects from your muscles. It's like your body's safety switch, preventing you from physically acting out your dreams. The pontine tegmentum orchestrates this too, ensuring you remain safely in bed while your mind explores dreamscapes.

Your brain's activity during REM sleep might surprise you. Despite being asleep, parts of your brain become more active than when you're awake. The visual cortex lights up with activity, explaining the rich imagery in your dreams. Meanwhile, areas involved in logical thinking become less active, which is why dreams often defy real-world logic.

Throughout the night, you cycle through REM and non-REM sleep multiple times. Each REM period typically becomes longer as the night progresses, like chapters in a book growing more detailed. Your first REM period might last only 10 minutes, while later ones can stretch to an hour or more.

Understanding REM sleep's role in mental health might be one of the most crucial aspects of dream science. Think of REM sleep as your brain's emotional maintenance crew, working the night shift to process the day's emotional experiences.

During REM sleep, your brain actively processes emotional memories. The amygdala - your emotional control center - becomes highly active, while the prefrontal cortex - responsible for logical thinking - takes a step back. This unique state allows your brain to process difficult emotions without the interference of rational thought, like having a therapeutic session with yourself while you sleep.

Have you ever noticed how a good night's sleep helps you feel more emotionally balanced? Studies show that REM sleep helps regulate mood by reducing the emotional intensity of difficult memories. It's like your brain is running an overnight emotional detox program, helping you wake up feeling more emotionally resilient.

But what happens when this natural process gets disrupted? REM sleep deprivation can have serious consequences for your psychological well-being. People who consistently miss out on REM sleep often report increased anxiety, difficulty concentrating, and mood swings. It's like trying to run your computer without ever clearing its cache - eventually, things start to malfunction.

Research has shown a strong link between REM sleep disruption and various mental health conditions. People with depression often show abnormal REM sleep patterns, either getting too much or too little. Similarly, anxiety disorders frequently co-occur with REM sleep disturbances, creating a challenging cycle where emotional distress disrupts sleep, and poor sleep worsens emotional distress.

Your brain needs adequate REM sleep to maintain emotional balance. During REM, your brain processes and integrates emotional experiences, helping you adapt to life's challenges. Without this crucial processing time, you might find yourself more reactive to stress and less able to cope with emotional situations.

Beyond emotional processing, REM sleep plays a crucial role in keeping your cognitive abilities sharp. Think of your brain during REM sleep as a master librarian, carefully organizing and storing important information from your day.

During REM sleep, your brain strengthens neural connections - the pathways that help you remember and learn. Scientists call this process synaptic consolidation. It's like your brain is building bridges between different pieces of information, making them easier to access later. This explains why studying right before bed often helps with retention - your brain uses REM sleep to cement that new knowledge into long-term memory.

Ever wonder why sleeping on a problem often leads to a solution? Research backs this up. In one fascinating experiment, participants were given complex puzzles to solve. Those who got REM sleep between attempts performed significantly better than those who stayed awake. Your brain continues working on problems even while you sleep, making new connections and finding creative solutions.

Studies show that people who get adequate REM sleep perform better on memory tests and creative thinking tasks. During REM, your brain rehearses and strengthens the neural pathways created during learning. It's like practicing a new skill in a virtual environment - the more you practice during REM sleep, the better you become at performing that skill when awake.

But here's what makes REM sleep truly special for learning: it's the only time when your brain produces specific waves that support memory formation. These waves, called theta waves, help transfer information from your hippocampus (where short-term memories live) to your neocortex (where long-term memories are stored). Without this transfer process, much of what you learn during the day would be lost.

Scientists have observed this process using brain imaging technology. During REM sleep, areas of the brain involved in learning and memory light up with activity. It's as if your brain is running a sophisticated backup program, ensuring important information gets saved properly.

While REM sleep is crucial for our well-being, some people struggle with conditions that disrupt this vital process. REM sleep disorders can significantly impact both the quality of sleep and overall health.

REM Behavior Disorder (RBD) stands out as one of the most dramatic sleep conditions. Unlike typical REM sleep where your body remains still while your mind dreams, people with RBD physically act out their dreams. A person might punch, kick, or jump out of bed while sound asleep.

These episodes can be dangerous for both the person affected and their bed partner. Simple safety measures like padding the floor around the bed or using bed rails become necessary. What makes RBD particularly concerning is its association with certain neurological conditions - it can sometimes appear years before other symptoms develop.

Sleep apnea presents another challenge to healthy REM sleep. This condition causes repeated breathing interruptions throughout the night, preventing people from reaching or maintaining proper REM sleep. Each time breathing stops, the brain jolts partially awake, disrupting the natural sleep cycle.

People with sleep apnea often have fragmented, chaotic dreams or difficulty remembering their dreams at all. It's like trying to watch a movie while someone keeps hitting pause every few minutes - you never get the full story.

The consequences of disrupted REM sleep reach far beyond simple daytime fatigue. Without proper REM cycles, the brain struggles to perform its essential maintenance and processing functions. During work or study, concentration wavers as the mind fights to stay focused - similar to trying to read through foggy glasses. Tasks that once seemed manageable become overwhelming challenges.

Emotional regulation suffers significantly when REM sleep is compromised. The brain loses its ability to process daily experiences and emotions effectively. This manifests as unexpected mood swings, from sudden irritability to feelings of overwhelm at minor setbacks. The emotional landscape becomes unpredictable, affecting both personal and professional relationships.

Creative thinking and problem-solving abilities decline sharply with poor REM sleep. The mind loses its capacity to make novel connections or approach challenges from different angles. Solutions that might typically come naturally remain frustratingly out of reach. This impacts everything from workplace innovation to daily troubleshooting tasks.

Perhaps most concerning is the effect on memory formation. The brain requires REM sleep to convert short-term memories into long-term storage. Without this crucial process, new information slips away like water through fingers. Important details from meetings, conversations, or learning experiences fail to stick, creating gaps in knowledge and understanding. This creates a cumulative effect where each day of disrupted REM sleep adds to an expanding deficit of properly stored memories and processed information.

Treatment options exist for both conditions. RBD often responds well to medication, while sleep apnea typically improves with CPAP therapy or other breathing devices. The key lies in recognizing the symptoms and seeking proper medical evaluation.

2

Brain Waves and Dream Formation

L et's dive into the fascinating world of brain waves during sleep. If you've ever wondered why some dreams feel vivid while others slip away like smoke, understanding these patterns can unlock the mystery.

Think of your brain as an orchestra, with different instruments playing at various frequencies. During our waking hours, beta waves dominate - these are the fast-paced rhythms of daily life, humming along at 12-38 Hz. Picture yourself answering emails or solving problems at work - that's beta in action.

As you begin to relax, perhaps curling up with this book, alpha waves take over. Running at 8-12 Hz, these waves create that peaceful state where your thoughts start to drift. It's like that moment when you're gazing out a window, not quite daydreaming but not fully focused either.

Theta waves (4-8 Hz) emerge as you drift closer to sleep. This is where things get interesting - these waves often bring those strange, fleeting images just before you doze off. You might suddenly see yourself flying or falling, only to jerk awake wondering where that came from.

Delta waves, the slowest at 0.5-4 Hz, signal deep sleep. These powerful waves sweep through your brain like slow, rolling thunder. While we typically don't remember dreams from this stage, these waves play a crucial role in resetting your brain for another day.

Each of these wave patterns contributes uniquely to our dream experiences. The shift between them isn't like flipping a switch - it's more like a dance, with each pattern flowing into the next. Understanding these patterns helps explain why some nights deliver vivid adventure movies while others leave us with only vague impressions come morning.

You don't need a PhD to appreciate how these waves shape your dream life. Simply knowing they exist can help you better understand your own sleep experiences. Next time you're lying in bed, drifting off, you might notice the subtle shift as your brain transitions from the busy beta of daily life to the gentler rhythms that guide you into the dream world.

Let's explore how theta waves influence your dreams - particularly why some mornings you wake up with crystal-clear memories while other dreams fade like morning mist.

Theta waves create a fascinating bridge between wakefulness and sleep. Running at 4-8 Hz, these waves dominate during REM sleep when most vivid dreams occur. Think of theta waves as your brain's storytelling rhythm - they help weave together the narratives and imagery that make up your dreams.

"But why can I remember some dreams perfectly while others slip away?" This is one of the most common questions dreamers have. The answer lies in how theta waves interact with different parts of your brain during REM sleep. When theta waves are strong and consistent, they help forge stronger connections between your hippocampus (where memories form) and your cortex (where we process experiences).

Studies show people with more prominent theta activity during REM sleep tend to remember their dreams more clearly. It's like having a better signal strength when recording a video - clearer signal, clearer playback.

You might notice some mornings you wake up with dreams so vivid they feel like memories of actual events. That's likely because your brain experienced strong theta wave activity during those dreams. These waves help stamp the dream experiences into your short-term memory, giving you that window of opportunity to write them down or reflect on them before they fade.

These brain wave patterns can help us better appreciate why our dream recall varies so much from night to night. Think of theta waves as your dream's preservation system - when they're working optimally, they help ensure your nighttime adventures don't vanish with the morning light.

Your brain's hemispheres dance together during sleep, creating a symphony that shapes your dreams. This synchronization isn't random - it's a precisely choreographed process that determines how vivid and memorable your dreams become. You may think dreams were just random firings in your brain but this is actually the work of hemispheric synchronization and it explains why some dreams feel so real and meaningful.

Recent studies reveal that during REM sleep, your brain's left and right hemispheres communicate more freely than when you're awake. The corpus callosum - the bridge between hemispheres - becomes highly active, allowing information to flow more smoothly between both sides of your brain.

This enhanced communication creates what researchers call "whole-brain experiences." Your analytical left hemisphere merges with your creative right hemisphere, explaining why dreams can be both logically structured yet wildly imaginative. It's like having your internal editor and artist working together without their usual daytime constraints.

Brain imaging studies show fascinating patterns during this process. When both hemispheres sync up strongly, people report more coherent dream narratives. Instead of fragmented scenes, they experience dreams with clear storylines and meaningful connections.

The synchronization varies throughout the night. Early REM periods typically show less hemispheric coordination, which might explain why early-night dreams often feel more chaotic. As the night progresses, the synchronization typically strengthens, leading to those vivid morning dreams that stick with you.

Think of your brain waves like musicians in an orchestra. When they play in harmony, you get beautiful music - or in this case, memorable dreams. When they're out of sync, the experience becomes harder to recall or make sense of.

Your brain is remarkably adaptable, constantly rewiring itself based on your experiences. This process, called neuroplasticity, plays a crucial role in how your dreams form and evolve. Think of your brain as a living map that updates itself every time you learn something new or face different challenges.

During sleep, your brain doesn't just replay memories - it actively reorganizes neural pathways. This restructuring helps you process daily experiences and adapt to changes in your environment. Dreams emerge from this reorganization, reflecting both recent events and deeper patterns stored in your neural networks.

"But why do some dreams feel so strange yet meaningful?" you might wonder. The answer lies in how your brain's plasticity allows it to form new connections during sleep. Your neural networks become more flexible, enabling unusual combinations of memories and emotions that create unique dream experiences.

Research shows that people who engage in new activities or learn new skills often dream about these experiences differently over time. At first, dreams might directly mirror the learning process. As your brain adapts and masters these skills, the dreams evolve, becoming more abstract and integrated with other memories.

This adaptability explains why recurring dreams can change as you grow and face new life challenges. Your brain's plastic nature allows dream content to shift, reflecting your personal growth and changing circumstances. It's like your mind is constantly updating its internal software through dreams.

Studies of people learning physical skills, like playing an instrument or mastering a sport, reveal fascinating patterns. Their brains show increased plasticity during sleep, particularly in areas related to the new skill. Their dreams often incorporate elements of practice, helping consolidate these new neural pathways.

For those dealing with emotional challenges or trauma, this plasticity becomes especially important. Dreams provide a safe space for your brain to process difficult experiences, forming new neural connections that can help with healing and adaptation. This is why dreams can feel like emotional problem-solving sessions - because in many ways, they are.

3

The Role of Memory in Dreams

Have you ever wondered why certain moments from your day pop up in your dreams? It's not a surprise that our daily experiences weave themselves into our nighttime narratives in amazing ways.

Picture this: You're having a casual conversation with a coworker about their new red car. That night, you dream about driving a crimson sports car through winding mountain roads. This isn't just coincidence - it's what dream researchers call the "day residue" effect. Your brain takes fragments of daily experiences and transforms them into dream material, often within 24-48 hours of the original event.

"But my dreams aren't exact copies of my day," you might say. You're absolutely right. Sigmund Freud called this process "dream-work" - the way our minds disguise and reshape memories into dream content. That stressful presentation at work might become a dream about performing on stage in your pajamas. Your brain isn't just replaying events; it's processing them, mixing them with older memories, and creating new connections.

Think about the last time you had a vivid dream that included people from different parts of your life meeting in impossible situations. Maybe your third-grade teacher was having coffee with your current boss. This bizarre mixing of memories shows how dreams don't follow the same rules as waking life - they create their own logic by blending various memory fragments.

Your brain doesn't just pick random memories to feature in dreams. Often, it selects experiences that carry emotional weight or need processing. That's why a small comment that bothered you might show up in an exaggerated form in your dreams, while major events sometimes don't appear at all. The mind is selective about what it chooses to explore during sleep.

Understanding this connection between memories and dreams helps explain why keeping a dream journal can be so revealing. When you track your dreams alongside daily events, patterns emerge. You start to see how your mind processes experiences and transforms them into dream material.

Dreams don't just replay our memories - they help cement them into our minds. While you sleep, your brain works overtime to process and store the day's experiences, like a librarian organizing books on shelves.

The hippocampus, that seahorse-shaped structure deep in your brain, plays a starring role in this nightly filing system. Think of it as your brain's memory coordinator. During sleep, it reviews recent experiences and transfers them from short-term to long-term storage. Have you ever noticed how a good night's sleep helps you remember things better? That's your hippocampus at work.

An example would be pulling an all-nighter studying session but feeling like you didn't retain much of the information. Research shows that sleep deprivation disrupts this vital memory consolidation process. When you skimp on sleep, you're essentially telling your brain to try filing papers in a tornado - it just doesn't work well.

Let's break this down with a real-world example. Say you're learning a new language. During the day, you practice vocabulary and grammar. At night, your sleeping brain replays these learning experiences, strengthening the neural connections that help you remember. This is why people often find they perform better on language tests after a solid night's sleep.

The connection between sleep and memory goes both ways. Just as sleep helps us remember, our ability to recall dreams improves when we're well-rested. It's like trying to take a clear photo - the steadier your hand (or in this case, the better your sleep), the sharper the image.

Studies show that people who maintain regular sleep schedules tend to remember their dreams more vividly. This isn't just about quantity of sleep - it's about quality. When your sleep cycles flow naturally, your brain has the best chance to process memories and generate dreams you can recall upon waking.

Your memory isn't just a recording device - it's more like a creative writing workshop where your brain edits, revises, and reorganizes information. Dreams are part of this process, helping to sort through the day's experiences and file them away where they belong.

Dreams aren't just replays of past events - they're also your brain's practice ground for future scenarios. Like a coach running drills before the big game, your mind uses dreams to rehearse potential situations and solutions. Research shows our brains use sleep to simulate challenging situations in a safe environment. It's like having your own virtual reality training program running while you rest. Your dreams create scenarios where your brain can practice without real consequences.

You may have heard of athletes who dream about their performances before a big game. Their sleeping brains run through movements, strategies, and potential obstacles. It's mental rehearsal on autopilot.

But these rehearsals aren't limited to specific skills or problems. Dreams can help us practice emotional responses too. Having anxiety about an upcoming presentation? Your dreams might put you in front of various audiences, letting you work through those nerves while you sleep.

Think of your dreaming mind as a simulator. Just as pilots use flight simulators to prepare for different situations, your brain uses dreams to ready itself for life's challenges. The scenarios might seem bizarre - maybe you're giving that presentation to a room full of penguins - but the emotional and problem-solving components are very real.

This memory rehearsal mechanism explains why we often dream about things we're worried about or working on. Your brain isn't just processing what happened - it's actively preparing for what might happen next.

When it comes to memories in dreams, things aren't always what they seem. Our dreams can twist and reshape memories in unexpected ways. You might dream about your childhood home, but find the layout completely different, or see people from different parts of your life inhabiting the same space.

These distortions aren't random glitches - they're part of how our brains process and store information. Just like a computer compressing files to save space, your brain sometimes combines or alters memories to make them fit. This is why dream memories can feel both familiar and strange at the same time.

Have you ever woken up convinced something happened, only to realize it was just a dream? This phenomenon, known as false memory formation, is more common than you might think. Dreams can feel so real that our brains sometimes file them away as actual memories. It's like saving a movie scene alongside your real-life experiences - they can get mixed up in storage.

Think about trying to remember a dream right after waking up. The details often slip away like water through your fingers. This isn't because you're forgetful - it's because dreams exist in a different state of consciousness. Your brain processes and stores dream memories differently than waking memories.

Let me share a common experience many people have: You wake up from a vivid dream, certain you'll remember every detail. But by breakfast, key elements start to fade. By lunch, you might only recall fragments. This isn't a failure of memory - it's your brain's natural filtering process at work.

The relationship between dreams and memory isn't a one-way street. While memories influence our dreams, dreams can also influence how we remember things. Sometimes, what we think we remember about past events might actually be colored by our dreams about them.

For those of you keeping dream journals, you might notice this happening. What you write down immediately after waking might feel crystal clear, but when you read it later, you might wonder if that's really what happened in the dream. This isn't a sign of poor recall - it's a normal part of how our brains handle dream memories.

4

Sleep Cycles and Dream Patterns

E ver wondered why some dreams feel like epic adventures while others slip away before you can remember them? The secret lies in understanding how our sleep works. Knowing your sleep stages is like having a map to your dream world.

Let's break it down into something we can all understand. Think of your nightly sleep as a journey through different neighborhoods. First, you enter NREM (Non-Rapid Eye Movement) sleep - it's like the quiet suburbs of your mind. Your breathing slows, your muscles relax, and your brain waves start to change. This is where your body does its repair work, but don't think nothing's happening in your mind. Light dreams can occur here, though they're usually more like fleeting thoughts than full stories.

Then there's REM sleep - the bustling downtown of your dream world. This is where the magic happens. Your eyes dart around under your eyelids, your body becomes temporarily paralyzed, and your brain lights up with activity. Most of those vivid, story-like dreams you remember? They happen during REM.

But before you reach either of these stages, you pass through something fascinating called the hypnagogic state. It's like standing in the doorway between being awake and asleep. You might experience sudden jerks, hear phantom sounds, or see flashing lights or images. These aren't technically dreams, but they're often just as interesting. Some people report their best creative ideas during this state.

"But I never remember falling asleep," you might say. That's because the hypnagogic state is like trying to watch yourself blink - the moment you notice it happening, it's already changed. Still, this transition period is crucial for setting up your night of dreams.

Think of your sleep cycles like waves on the ocean - they rise and fall in a predictable pattern throughout the night. Each cycle takes about 90 to 120 minutes to complete. That means if you sleep for eight hours, you'll go through about 4-6 complete cycles.

Here's what happens in each cycle: You start in light sleep, Stage 1, where you're easily awakened. Your brain waves slow down from their daytime beta waves to gentler alpha waves. Then you drift deeper into Stage 2, where your body temperature drops and your heart rate slows. This is when those theta waves kick in - they're like the cleaning crew, helping sort through your day's experiences.

Next comes deep sleep, Stages 3 and 4, dominated by slow delta waves. Think of this as your body's maintenance time. You're less likely to dream here, but when you do, these dreams tend to be more thought-like than story-like.

Finally, you enter REM sleep, where most of your vivid dreams occur. During your first cycle, REM might only last 10 minutes. But here's the interesting part - each subsequent cycle typically has longer REM periods. By your final cycle of the night, you might spend up to an hour in REM sleep.

This pattern explains why dreams early in the night often feel brief and fragmented, while those closer to morning can feel like feature-length films. It's not your imagination - your dream length really does increase as the night progresses.

That's why you might wake up remembering a long, detailed dream right before your alarm goes off. You were likely in an extended REM period, the prime time for those epic dream adventures. Understanding this pattern can help you make sense of why some nights feel full of dreams while others seem dreamless - it often depends on which sleep stage you're in when you wake up.

Just like fingerprints, no two people dream exactly alike. Your personal sleep patterns are as unique as you are, shaped by countless factors from your age to your daily habits.

Think about how your dreams might differ from your grandmother's or your teenage cousin's. As we age, our sleep architecture - the blueprint of our sleep cycles - undergoes significant changes. Infants spend about 50% of their sleep in REM, which explains those twitching smiles during naptime. By adulthood, REM typically accounts for only 20-25% of total sleep time, and this percentage continues to decrease as we get older.

Your lifestyle plays a crucial role too. Night shift workers often experience fragmented sleep cycles, which can lead to shorter or less vivid dreams. Athletes might spend more time in deep sleep for physical recovery, potentially experiencing fewer remembered dreams. Students cramming for exams might notice more stress-related dreams during their irregular sleep schedules.

Even your preferred sleep position can influence your dream patterns. Back sleepers often report more frequent nightmares, while side sleepers tend to have more emotionally neutral dreams. These differences might stem from subtle changes in brain blood flow or breathing patterns.

Consider your natural chronotype - whether you're a night owl or early bird. Morning people often report more positive dream content, while night owls might experience more vivid or bizarre dreams. This could be related to variations in hormonal rhythms and stress levels throughout the day.

Your sleep environment matters too. Someone living in a noisy city might have more interrupted sleep cycles than someone in a quiet rural area. These environmental factors can lead to different dream experiences, even among people of the same age and lifestyle.

Remember, there's no "normal" when it comes to dream patterns. What works for your best friend might not work for you. Understanding your personal sleep cycle variations can help you make sense of your unique dream experiences.

Have you ever woken up with a vivid dream fresh in your mind, only to find it slipping away like morning mist? The timing of when you wake up plays a crucial role in whether you remember your dreams or not.

Going back to our ocean wave analogy, the best time to catch your dreams is at the crest of the wave - when you're naturally transitioning from REM sleep to a lighter sleep stage.

"But how do I know when that is?" you might ask.

Here's a practical approach: Start by calculating backward from your wake-up time. If you need to wake up at 7 AM, count back in 90-minute increments. This gives you potential wake-up times of 5:30 AM, 4 AM, 2:30 AM, and so on. Setting your alarm for one of these times increases your chances of waking during REM sleep, when dreams are most vivid.

Another strategy involves using sleep tracking apps. While not perfect, they can help identify your personal sleep patterns. Look for ones that monitor movement and sound, giving you a rough estimate of your sleep cycles.

The "five more minutes" habit actually works against dream recall. When you hit snooze, you're likely diving back into a new sleep cycle, making it harder to remember dreams from earlier cycles. Instead, when you first wake up, stay still. Keep your eyes closed. Let your mind drift back to any dream fragments. Only then, reach for your dream journal.

Some people find success with the "wake-back-to-bed" method. Set an alarm for about six hours after going to sleep, wake up for 15-30 minutes, then go back to sleep. This often leads to more conscious awareness during subsequent REM periods, making dreams easier to remember.

Remember those nights when stress keeps you tossing and turning? Irregular sleep patterns can disrupt your natural cycles, making dream recall more difficult. Maintaining consistent sleep and wake times helps stabilize your cycles, improving both sleep quality and dream recall.

5

The Language of Symbols in Dreams

Dreams speak in the language of symbols, much like how your phone buzzes to tell you someone's thinking of you. But unlike your phone's clear notifications, dream symbols aren't one-size-fits-all.

Think about water in dreams. You might see it as threatening if you once had a scary experience swimming, while someone else finds it peaceful because they grew up near the ocean. That's why those dream dictionaries gathering dust on your shelf often miss the mark - they ignore your personal connection to these symbols.

For example, you may dream about missing a train. A dream dictionary would say this means you're afraid of missing opportunities. But you don't use trains in your daily life, you drive everywhere. Your actual fear triggering this may be you're afraid of being late to pick up your kids from school.

This perfectly illustrates how our daily lives shape our dream symbols. Your subconscious pulls from your experiences, fears, and joys to create a unique symbolic language. That childhood teddy bear might represent comfort, while for someone else, stuffed animals trigger memories of loneliness.

Common symbols do exist - teeth falling out, being chased, flying. But their meanings shift based on your cultural background and life experiences. A snake might represent wisdom in one culture and danger in another. That's why understanding your dreams starts with understanding yourself.

Keep a dream journal, but don't just record the dreams. Note your emotional reactions. If you dream of a red door, write down what the color red means to you, what doors represent in your life. Maybe red reminds you of your grandmother's kitchen, or doors make you think of new opportunities.

Your dreams aren't puzzles to be solved with a universal key. They're personal messages encoded in symbols drawn from your life's experiences. Learning to interpret them means becoming fluent in your own symbolic language.

Throughout history, dreams have fascinated humanity, sparking rich traditions of interpretation across cultures. The ancient Egyptians saw dreams as divine messages, recording them in hieroglyphs on temple walls. Their dream interpreters held prestigious positions in pharaohs' courts, believing specific symbols carried universal meanings.

In the temples of Serapis people would sleep on special beds, hoping the gods would send healing dreams. They believed snakes represented wisdom and power - quite different from our modern fear-based interpretations.

The Greeks took dream interpretation further, establishing dream temples called Asclepions. Here, priests would guide visitors through ritual sleep sessions, interpreting their dreams for medical diagnosis and treatment. They viewed dreams as direct communications from their gods, particularly Apollo and Asclepius.

But perhaps most fascinating are indigenous cultures' approaches to dream symbols. Unlike our modern tendency to seek fixed meanings, many Native American tribes view dreams as journeys of the soul.

For example, a Native American may dream of an eagle. Our Western interpretation of this may be about leadership or freedom. But to a Native American, the eagle may be their spirit guide trying to show them something specific to their life path.

The Australian Aboriginals maintain their ancestral tradition of Dreamtime - where dreams aren't separate from waking reality but form an integral part of their spiritual and physical world. Their dream symbols often connect to the land itself, carrying stories passed down through generations.

These diverse cultural perspectives remind us that dream symbols aren't universal. What meant death to one civilization might represent rebirth to another. The Egyptian ankh symbol appearing in your dreams might not carry the same significance as it did for ancient dream interpreters - your personal associations matter more than historical meanings.

This rich tapestry of cultural dream interpretation shows us that while we can learn from historical perspectives, our modern understanding needs to embrace personal and cultural contexts rather than seeking absolute meanings in ancient practices.

While ancient cultures offer fascinating perspectives on dream symbols, your personal dream symbols matter most. Think of them as your mind's unique language - a private dictionary built from your experiences, fears, hopes, and memories. Once you connect your personal history to the context of your dreams, your dreams will start to make more sense.

Starting a dream journal helps uncover these personal symbols. Keep it simple - a notebook by your bed or a notes app on your phone. Record not just the symbols, but your immediate emotional reactions. Did that red door fill you with dread or curiosity? Was the ocean peaceful or threatening?

Try this exercise: Pick a recurring symbol from your dreams and write down your first three associations. A house might represent safety to one person but feel like a trap to another. There are no wrong answers - your associations are uniquely yours.

Pay attention to patterns. When exploring your symbols, consider:

- What memories does this symbol trigger?

- How do you feel when you encounter it in waking life?

- Does it remind you of someone or something from your past?

Create a symbol map in your journal. Draw the main symbol in the center and branch out with connected emotions, memories, and life events. This visual approach often reveals connections you might miss through writing alone. Don't get hung up on traditional dream dictionaries. Create your own dictionary complete with symbols from your dream and the personal meaning they have to you.

The key is acknowledging that no single interpretation system holds all the answers. Your cultural background provides an important lens for understanding your dreams, but it's just one piece of the puzzle. Consider how your family traditions, religious beliefs, and cultural experiences shape the way you view symbols in both your waking life and dreams.

6

Archetypes: Universal Themes in Dreaming

The human psyche contains universal patterns and symbols that transcend cultural boundaries - these are what Carl Jung termed archetypes. Like ancient templates embedded in our collective unconscious, archetypes appear in dreams as recognizable characters and motifs that carry deep psychological significance.

Jung proposed that archetypes represent fundamental human experiences and emotional needs that have been present throughout our evolutionary history. When these primal patterns emerge in dreams, they often take familiar forms: the wise elder offering guidance, the trickster creating chaos, or the mother figure providing nurture. These aren't just random dream characters, but manifestations of core aspects of human nature.

The hero archetype frequently appears in dreams during times of personal challenge or growth. This might manifest as climbing a mountain, slaying a dragon, or leading others through danger. The hero represents our innate drive to overcome obstacles and transform ourselves. When this archetype surfaces in dreams, it often signals a period of necessary change or evolution in the dreamer's life.

The shadow archetype represents the parts of ourselves we reject or refuse to acknowledge - our "dark side." In dreams, the shadow might appear as a threatening figure, a monster, or even a person we strongly dislike. Encountering the shadow in dreams provides an opportunity to recognize and integrate these denied aspects of ourselves.

The Great Mother archetype manifests in dreams as a powerful feminine force, embodying both creative and destructive aspects of nature. She appears not only as a biological mother but as any nurturing presence - perhaps as Mother Earth, a goddess figure, or even a garden bursting with life. In dreams, she might emerge as a warm, protective force during times of vulnerability, offering comfort through symbols like a warm embrace or a sheltering tree.

However, the Great Mother also has a dark aspect. When this emerges in dreams, it might appear as a smothering presence or an overwhelming force of nature like a flood or storm. These dreams often surface when we're grappling with dependency issues or feeling consumed by responsibilities. The appearance of the negative mother archetype can signal a need to establish boundaries or break free from overwhelming situations.

The Wise Old Man or Woman represents our connection to inner wisdom and spiritual guidance. In dreams, this archetype might appear as a teacher, mentor, doctor, or spiritual guide. They often emerge during periods of difficult decisions or spiritual seeking, offering guidance through symbols or direct knowledge.

This archetype commonly manifests in dreams through familiar cultural images - a wizard with a long beard, an elderly indigenous healer, or a mysterious librarian surrounded by ancient books. Their presence typically signals a need to look beyond surface-level solutions and tap into deeper wisdom. The setting often reflects this theme, with the Wise One appearing in libraries, mountaintops, or sacred spaces.

The Wise Elder's guidance in dreams rarely comes as direct instructions. Instead, they might present riddles, show symbolic objects, or lead the dreamer through meaningful landscapes. These dreams often occur when the conscious mind has reached its limits in solving a problem, suggesting that answers lie in accessing deeper intuitive knowledge.

The appearance of either archetype in dreams invites careful reflection rather than immediate action. Their presence suggests engaging with the deeper meanings and patterns underlying current life situations rather than seeking quick solutions.

The Child archetype appears in dreams as a symbol of new beginnings and untapped potential. During periods of personal growth or when facing opportunities for fresh starts, this archetype might manifest as a literal child, a small animal, or even a sprouting plant. The Child represents our capacity for wonder and trust in life's unfolding. In dreams where this archetype emerges, pay attention to the child's emotional state - a joyful child suggests alignment with new possibilities, while a neglected child might indicate ignored opportunities or creative projects requiring attention.

The Trickster brings an element of creative chaos into dreams, often appearing when established patterns need disruption. This archetype might take the form of a clever animal like a fox or coyote, a street performer, or even a technological glitch. Trickster dreams frequently occur during times when questioning authority or breaking free from conventional thinking becomes necessary. The Trickster's presence can signal the need to approach problems from unexpected angles or challenge self-imposed limitations.

The Anima/Animus represents the integration of feminine and masculine energies within each person, regardless of gender. In dreams, the Anima often appears to men as a mysterious woman, perhaps as a dancer, artist, or nature spirit, representing connection to emotions and intuition. The Animus appears to females as a man of action or intellect - perhaps a warrior, professor, or explorer - representing qualities of logic and assertiveness.

These complementary archetypes tend to surface in dreams during periods of personal growth, particularly when developing underutilized aspects of personality. Their appearance often coincides with relationship challenges or questions of identity, suggesting the need to integrate different aspects of self. The state of these figures in dreams - whether harmonious or in conflict - can reflect one's current relationship with these internal energies.

Archetypal symbols in dreams serve as powerful catalysts for personal growth, offering a universal language that speaks directly to our unconscious mind. Working with archetypal dreams requires careful attention to personal associations and emotional responses. A dream journal tracking archetypal appearances can reveal patterns in personal development.

These archetypal patterns transcend cultural boundaries while maintaining individual relevance. The same dream symbol - like a wise elder offering guidance - carries universal meaning yet takes on personal significance based on one's life experience and current challenges. Understanding these archetypal elements provides a framework for interpreting dreams' deeper messages about personal growth and transformation. These archetypal patterns help decode the universal language of dreams. While personal and cultural contexts always influence dream interpretation, recognizing archetypal elements reveals deeper layers of meaning rooted in our shared human experience.

7

Interpreting Emotions Through Dream Scenarios

Dreams serve as mirrors reflecting our deepest emotional states, often bringing unprocessed feelings to the surface during sleep. These emotional themes emerge through vivid imagery and scenarios that connect directly to our waking concerns, fears, and unresolved conflicts.

Fear-based dreams commonly manifest through universal scenarios - falling from heights, being chased, or finding oneself unprepared for an important event. These dreams typically point to underlying anxieties about loss of control, vulnerability, or performance pressure in daily life. A dream about being pursued may reveal avoidance of a pressing issue, while showing up naked to an important meeting often reflects feelings of exposure or impostor syndrome in professional settings.

The intensity of fear in these dreams often correlates with the significance of the underlying emotional trigger. Someone experiencing workplace stress might dream of being trapped in an elevator or lost in an endless maze of office corridors. These scenarios amplify the emotional experience, forcing acknowledgment of fears that may be minimized during waking hours.

Dreams of loss carry particularly powerful emotional resonance, touching on fundamental human fears of abandonment, death, and change. Common manifestations include searching for lost objects, missing loved ones, or being unable to find one's way home. The lost object often symbolizes something beyond its literal representation - a missing wallet might represent concerns about security or identity, while a lost phone could reflect anxiety about connection and communication.

The emotional impact of loss dreams tends to linger upon waking, creating a visceral reminder of unaddressed grief or uncertainty. These dreams frequently surface during periods of transition - career changes, relationship endings, or major life decisions - when the psyche processes the emotional weight of real or anticipated losses.

The timing and frequency of these emotional dreams often align with significant life events or periods of stress, serving as indicators of which aspects of our emotional lives require attention and processing. Regular patterns of anxiety dreams or recurring loss scenarios point to persistent unresolved feelings that may benefit from conscious examination.

Dreams often carry emotional weight that extends beyond their surface narrative. By exploring these emotions through active engagement techniques, we can better understand their connection to our waking lives. Role-playing offers a powerful method to decode the emotional landscape of our dreams.

Consider a dream where you're giving a presentation but your voice won't work. Instead of dismissing this as a simple anxiety dream, try standing up and physically recreating the scenario. Notice where tension manifests in your body. Does your throat tighten? Do your hands shake? These physical responses often mirror real-life situations where you feel silenced or powerless.

Another technique involves embodying different elements from your dream. In a dream about being lost in a dark forest, take time to "become" the forest itself. How does it feel to be vast, dark, and mysterious? Then shift to experiencing yourself as the lost wanderer. This perspective-switching can reveal hidden emotional dynamics at play in your life.

Movement-based exploration adds another dimension to dream interpretation. If you dream of flying, try expressing that sensation through gentle swaying or stretching. The physical expression often triggers emotional memories or associations that connect to current life situations where you're seeking freedom or transcendence.

For recurring dreams, create a dedicated space to physically reenact the scenario. A dream about being chased might lead you to actually run in place, allowing your body to process the fight-or-flight response. Pay attention to when your heart rate increases or where you feel the urge to hide. These physiological responses often point to similar patterns in your daily life where you feel pursued by obligations or responsibilities.

Role-playing techniques work best when approached with curiosity rather than judgment. There's no "correct" way to feel during these exercises. The goal is simply to notice what emotions arise and how they might reflect your waking experiences. Keep a journal nearby to record insights that emerge during these explorations.

Dreams serve as powerful windows into our emotional landscape, offering unique opportunities for healing and personal growth. When we experience intense emotions in dreams - whether fear, joy, anger, or sadness - these feelings often mirror unresolved issues in our waking lives. By paying attention to these dream emotions, we can gain valuable insights for our therapeutic journey.

Consider a recurring dream of being unprepared for an important test. The anxiety and panic felt during this dream may reflect deeper fears about performance, self-worth, or life transitions. In cognitive-behavioral therapy, this dream scenario becomes a starting point for examining thought patterns and beliefs that fuel these anxieties.

Dream emotions also provide safe spaces to process trauma. A person who experienced a car accident might dream of driving again, allowing them to work through their fear in the contained environment of their dreamscape. These dreams can gradually decrease in intensity as the emotional processing occurs, marking progress in the healing journey.

The therapeutic value of dreams extends to grief processing. Dreams of deceased loved ones often carry intense emotions that help us work through loss. While these dreams may initially feel painful, they frequently evolve to become sources of comfort and acceptance as emotional healing progresses.

Cognitive-behavioral therapy (CBT) techniques can harness dream emotions through several approaches. Dream reframing helps identify and challenge negative thought patterns that emerge in dreams. For instance, a dream about public humiliation might reveal underlying beliefs about social acceptance that can be addressed in therapy.

Dreams of being chased or attacked often signal avoidance behaviors in waking life. By examining these dream emotions through a CBT lens, individuals can develop strategies to face rather than flee from challenging situations. The emotional intensity of these dreams provides motivation for behavioral change.

Anxiety dreams commonly feature emotions of helplessness or lack of control. CBT practitioners can use these dream scenarios to help clients identify triggers and develop coping mechanisms. The vivid emotional content of dreams makes them particularly effective tools for recognizing anxiety patterns and practicing stress management techniques.

Strong emotions act as powerful amplifiers in our dream experiences, intensifying both the vivid nature of dreams and our ability to recall them upon waking. Research consistently shows that dreams carrying high emotional charge - whether positive or negative - tend to stick in our memory longer than neutral dream content.

The brain processes emotions differently during sleep compared to wakefulness. During REM sleep, the amygdala - our emotional processing center - becomes highly active while the prefrontal cortex that normally regulates emotions shows reduced activity. This creates an environment where emotions flow more freely, unrestrained by our usual rational controls.

Consider a dream about public speaking. For someone with social anxiety, this scenario typically generates intense feelings of fear or embarrassment. These heightened emotions trigger increased neural activity, making the dream more vivid and memorable. The physical sensations - racing heart, sweaty palms, shallow breathing - often feel as real as in waking life.

Positive emotions equally influence dream intensity. Dreams of joyful reunions, accomplishments, or falling in love create strong neural pathways through the release of feel-good neurotransmitters. These dreams frequently remain clear in our memory, sometimes persisting for years.

The correlation between emotional arousal and dream recall appears strongest when the emotions align with current life situations. A person going through relationship difficulties may experience more intense and memorable dreams about relationships. Their brain actively processes these emotions during sleep, leading to increased dream vividness and recall.

Studies tracking dream journals reveal that approximately 70-95% of remembered dreams contain some form of emotional content. Dreams rated as highly emotional are reported with greater frequency and detail compared to emotionally neutral dreams. This suggests our brain prioritizes the storage and recall of emotionally significant dream experiences.

Stress and anxiety particularly impact dream intensity. During periods of high stress, many people report more frequent and vivid nightmares or anxiety dreams. These dreams often feature enhanced sensory details and complex narratives, making them more memorable upon waking.

8

How the Subconscious Communicates Warnings

Dreams often act as our mind's early warning system, alerting us to potential dangers or issues we might overlook in our waking hours. Like a sophisticated alarm system, our subconscious processes subtle cues and patterns, weaving them into dream scenarios that demand our attention.

Recurring nightmares frequently signal underlying stress that needs addressing. A professional experiencing repeated dreams of showing up unprepared for meetings might be wrestling with imposter syndrome or work-related anxiety. The dream serves as a mirror, reflecting deep-seated fears about competence or performance that require acknowledgment.

The subconscious mind excels at pattern recognition, often picking up on relationship dynamics before our conscious mind catches up. Dreams of a partner becoming distant or turning into a stranger can indicate growing relationship tensions. These dreams might manifest when subtle changes in communication patterns or emotional availability occur, even before obvious signs of conflict emerge.

Physical health warnings can also appear in dreams. Dreams of suffocation or drowning might signal sleep apnea or respiratory issues. Teeth falling out - a common dream motif - often correlates with periods of heightened stress or anxiety about personal appearance and social standing.

The protective function of dreams extends beyond individual concerns to social relationships. Dreams about betrayal or abandonment might reflect picked-up social cues about shifting loyalties or changing dynamics within friend groups. The subconscious mind processes these subtle signals, presenting them through dream scenarios that prompt conscious awareness and potential preventive action.

Environmental threats might trigger protective dream responses too. Dreams about natural disasters often spike during periods of climate anxiety or after exposure to environmental news. These dreams serve as psychological preparation mechanisms, helping process and respond to potential threats.

Financial stress commonly manifests in dreams about loss or scarcity. Dreams of empty wallets, broken possessions, or being unable to pay for necessities might emerge during periods of economic uncertainty, prompting closer attention to financial planning and security.

Dreams often communicate through symbolic warnings, using universal imagery that resonates across cultures and individual experiences. These warning symbols act as messengers from our subconscious, highlighting areas of concern that require attention in our waking lives.

Water appears frequently as a powerful symbol of emotional states. Turbulent oceans or flooding often reflect overwhelming emotions or situations threatening to surge out of control. Murky or dark water might indicate hidden emotional depths or unclear feelings about a situation. A tsunami approaching in dreams frequently corresponds with anticipation of major life changes or emotional upheaval. Drowning in deep water commonly surfaces during periods of feeling emotionally overwhelmed at work or in relationships.

Clear, calm water typically represents emotional clarity or peace, making its opposite - choppy or stormy waters - a warning sign of brewing emotional turmoil. Dreams of being caught in a rainstorm often emerge during times of emotional release or when tears need to be shed. Standing water or stagnant pools might warn of emotional situations that have become toxic or require movement to resolve.

Falling dreams rank among the most common warning symbols, typically emerging when we feel our grip on some aspect of life slipping. The sensation of falling without a landing point often correlates with career uncertainty or major life transitions where the outcome remains unclear. Dreams of falling from specific heights - like buildings or cliffs - might signal fear of failure in particular projects or relationships.

The context of falling matters significantly. Falling in darkness often points to fear of the unknown, while falling in familiar places might indicate losing control in well-established situations. The feeling of falling while walking or standing suggests a loss of confidence or stable footing in daily life. Falling after being pushed could signal feelings of betrayal or external forces threatening stability.

These warning symbols tend to appear more frequently during periods of significant life changes or stress, serving as the mind's way of processing uncertainty and preparing for potential challenges. The intensity and frequency of these dreams often correlate with the urgency of the underlying concern requiring attention.

Personal warning signs in dreams often carry unique significance based on individual experiences and emotions. Unlike universal symbols, these personal signals emerge from our specific life circumstances, memories, and fears. Understanding these warnings requires consistent observation and reflection.

A dream journal serves as the cornerstone for identifying personal warning patterns. Keep it within arm's reach of your bed, along with a pen and small light. Upon waking, record every detail you remember, no matter how insignificant it seems. Include dates, times, and any significant events from the previous day. Pay special attention to recurring elements - they often point to unresolved issues demanding attention.

Structure your journal entries with specific sections. Start with the dream narrative, followed by prominent emotions felt during the dream. Note physical sensations - racing heart, sweating, tension - as these bodily responses often accompany warning dreams. List key symbols or objects that stood out, and record your initial interpretations while the dream remains fresh.

Look for patterns in your entries over time. Warning dreams tend to cluster around periods of stress or significant life changes. They might feature recurring locations, objects, or situations that hold personal meaning. For example, dreams of your childhood home might surface before major life transitions, serving as a warning about security concerns.

Review your journal weekly to identify these patterns. Create a simple tracking system - perhaps different colored highlighters for various themes or symbols. This visual approach helps spot connections between dream warnings and real-life events. Note when certain dreams precede specific situations, as this builds understanding of your personal warning system.

Consider creating a separate section for "warning dream indicators" - elements that consistently appear before challenging situations in your life. These might include specific weather conditions in dreams, particular animals, or recurring scenarios. By documenting these patterns, you develop a personal dictionary of warning signs unique to your dream language.

Dream warnings often surface through subtle patterns rather than dramatic revelations. Your subconscious mind processes thousands of environmental cues daily, picking up potential threats your conscious mind might miss. These warnings manifest in dreams, offering valuable insights for personal safety and decision-making.

Consider the case of recurring dreams about locked doors that won't secure properly. This common pattern may indicate vulnerability in your personal boundaries or living situation. Rather than dismissing such dreams, examine your home security, workplace dynamics, or relationship boundaries.

The dream highlights what your intuition already knows - something needs strengthening in your personal security system.

Dreams of being unprepared - showing up naked to work or missing an important exam - often precede situations where you're actually underprepared. These warnings prompt practical action: double-checking project deadlines, reviewing presentation materials, or ensuring important documents are in order. By heeding these dream signals, you can prevent real-world mishaps.

Environmental hazards frequently appear in warning dreams through symbolic representations. Dreams of water damage might prompt inspection of your home's plumbing. Dreams of electrical problems could suggest checking wiring or updating smoke detectors. Your brain processes subtle signs of deterioration during waking hours, presenting them more dramatically in dreams to capture your attention.

Vehicle-related dreams often reflect concerns about your life's direction or control. Dreams of brake failure, for instance, might indicate you're moving too fast in a business venture or relationship. Rather than ignoring these warnings, use them as prompts to reassess your pace and ensure proper precautions are in place.

Pay attention to dreams featuring unusual behavior from familiar people. If you dream of trusted colleagues acting suspiciously, examine your work relationships more closely. Your subconscious might be picking up on subtle changes in body language or communication patterns that warrant attention.

9

Lucid Dreaming: Mastering Awareness

L ucid dreaming opens a gateway to conscious exploration within the dream state, offering a unique opportunity to actively participate in and shape our dream experiences. Unlike regular dreams where we remain passive observers, lucid dreaming allows us to recognize we're dreaming while the dream unfolds. This awareness transforms the dream landscape into a laboratory for personal growth and creative discovery.

During lucid dreams, the mind maintains its analytical capabilities while accessing the unlimited creative potential of the dream state. Imagine gaining the ability to deliberately practice skills, experiment with new ideas, or work through complex problems - all within the safe confines of your mind. Athletes report improved performance after practicing movements in lucid dreams, while artists find inspiration by actively exploring vibrant dreamscapes their unconscious mind creates.

The benefits extend beyond creativity and skill enhancement. Lucid dreaming provides a powerful tool for confronting fears and anxieties in a controlled environment. Those struggling with recurring nightmares can learn to recognize dream signs and transform threatening scenarios into empowering experiences. This practice builds confidence that often carries over into waking life.

Problem-solving takes on new dimensions in lucid dreams. The brain, freed from physical constraints and logical limitations, can explore unconventional solutions. Scientists, inventors, and entrepreneurs have credited lucid dreams with breakthrough insights. The dream state allows the mind to test possibilities without real-world consequences, leading to innovative approaches that might otherwise remain undiscovered.

Research indicates that regular lucid dreamers exhibit enhanced self-reflection and metacognition - the ability to think about their own thinking processes. This heightened awareness often translates to improved decision-making and emotional intelligence in daily life. Additionally, studies suggest that lucid dreaming can reduce anxiety, improve sleep quality, and boost overall psychological well-being.

For those seeking personal growth, lucid dreaming offers a direct path to self-exploration. The practice allows individuals to engage with different aspects of their personality, confront limiting beliefs, and experiment with new behaviors in a consequence-free environment.

Achieving lucidity in dreams requires consistent practice and dedication to specific techniques that bridge the gap between waking consciousness and dream awareness. Reality checks serve as the foundation for developing lucid dreaming skills. Throughout the day, pause to question whether you're dreaming by examining your surroundings. Push against a wall, look at your hands, or try to read text twice - in dreams, these actions often yield inconsistent results. The key lies in making these checks habitual, performing them 10-15 times daily until they become second nature.

The hands technique proves particularly effective - examine your palms regularly during waking hours. In dreams, hands often appear distorted, with extra fingers or blurred details. This simple act, when performed consistently, trains the mind to carry this questioning awareness into dreams.

Digital displays and text provide another reliable reality check. In dreams, numbers and letters tend to shift or become illegible when viewed multiple times. Develop the habit of reading signs or checking your phone, then looking away and reading again. This practice increases the likelihood of recognizing dream signs during sleep.

The MILD technique (Mnemonic Induction of Lucid Dreams) builds on these foundation skills. Before sleep, set a clear intention to recognize when you're dreaming. Recall a recent dream in detail, identifying specific dream signs that could have triggered lucidity. Then, visualize yourself back in that dream, but this time becoming aware it's a dream. Repeat a simple phrase like "Next time I'm dreaming, I'll remember I'm dreaming" while holding this intention.

MILD works best when combined with the wake-back-to-bed method. Set an alarm for 5-6 hours after bedtime, when REM sleep occurs most frequently. Upon waking, stay alert for 10-15 minutes while focusing on your intention to achieve lucidity. This timing takes advantage of the brain's natural sleep cycles, increasing the chances of entering a lucid dream state.

These techniques require patience and persistence. Most practitioners report success after several weeks of consistent practice, though individual results vary. The key lies in maintaining regular reality checks and setting clear intentions before sleep.

Common challenges in lucid dreaming often arise just as awareness dawns within the dream state. The excitement of realizing you're dreaming can trigger an immediate return to wakefulness, disrupting the experience before it truly begins. To prevent this, practice emotional regulation techniques like deep breathing and gentle awareness during reality checks. When lucidity occurs, resist the urge to celebrate or analyze - simply observe and continue participating in the dream scenario.

Dream stability presents another significant hurdle. The dreamscape may blur, fade, or collapse once lucidity is achieved. Engaging your senses within the dream helps maintain stability. Touch nearby surfaces, examine details in your environment, or rub your dream hands together. These actions ground your awareness within the dream state and prevent premature awakening.

Visual clarity often fluctuates during lucid dreams. Dark or hazy scenes can be brightened by verbal commands like "increase clarity" or by imagining lights turning on. Spinning in place within the dream can also reset and stabilize a fading dreamscape. The key lies in maintaining a calm, confident approach - any anxiety or forceful attempts to control the dream typically lead to awakening.

False awakenings frequently occur during lucid dream attempts. You may think you've woken up, only to discover you're still dreaming. Perform reality checks whenever you wake up, especially after attempting lucid dreaming. This habit helps identify false awakenings and can transform them into new opportunities for lucidity.

Dream control requires balance. Attempting too much control too quickly often destabilizes the dream state. Start with small changes - altering objects or moving through space - before attempting more dramatic transformations. Build confidence gradually through successful minor adjustments before attempting more ambitious manipulations.

Sleep paralysis sometimes accompanies lucid dream attempts, particularly when using wake-induced techniques. Rather than fighting the sensation, remain calm and use it as a gateway to enter a lucid dream. Focus on floating or rolling out of your body while maintaining relaxed awareness.

Lucid dreaming offers powerful opportunities for confronting and overcoming personal limitations. Within the safe environment of a lucid dream, individuals can directly face their fears without real-world consequences. Someone afraid of public speaking might practice giving presentations in front of dream audiences, gradually building confidence through repeated exposure in this controlled setting.

Nightmare scenarios transform into growth opportunities when approached with lucid awareness. Rather than fleeing from threatening dream figures, lucid dreamers can turn and engage with these representations of their fears. A recurring nightmare about being chased might shift dramatically when the dreamer stops running and asks the pursuer what it represents.

Athletic performance benefits particularly well from lucid dream practice. Athletes can rehearse complex movements and perfect their form without physical strain or injury risk. A gymnast might practice a challenging routine repeatedly in the dream state, developing muscle memory and spatial awareness that transfers to waking performance.

Creative skills flourish through lucid dream exploration. Musicians can compose and practice new pieces, artists can experiment with impossible colors and perspectives, and writers can interact directly with their characters. These dream experiences often spark fresh insights that enhance waking creativity.

Problem-solving abilities sharpen through lucid dream practice. The dreaming mind can model different approaches to challenges without real-world limitations. Someone struggling with a work project might use lucid dreams to visualize various solutions, gaining new perspectives on the problem.

Emotional intelligence grows through intentional lucid dream interactions. Dreamers can practice difficult conversations, explore different emotional responses, and develop greater empathy by experiencing various perspectives within the dream. This emotional rehearsal builds confidence for handling challenging interpersonal situations in waking life.

10

The Power of Dream Journaling

A dream journal is more than just a notebook - it's a powerful tool for unlocking the mysteries of your subconscious mind. By keeping detailed records of your dreams, you create a personal archive that reveals patterns, recurring symbols, and emotional themes that might otherwise slip away into the morning fog.

The most effective dream journals combine quick-capture capabilities with space for deeper reflection. A simple two-column layout works well - use the left side for recording the raw dream experience immediately upon waking, and the right side for later analysis and interpretation. Include the date, time, and any notable events from the previous day that might have influenced the dream content.

Some journal formats incorporate symbol tracking sheets, where you can note recurring elements like water, flying, or specific colors. This helps identify personal dream patterns over time. Others include emotion scales to rate the intensity of feelings experienced during the dream, providing insight into your emotional landscape.

Digital journals offer searchability and tagging features, but many find that physically writing dreams helps with recall and processing. The act of putting pen to paper engages different neural pathways than typing, potentially strengthening memory formation. A hardbound notebook with quality paper can make the practice feel more meaningful and encourage consistent recording.

Consider including these elements in your dream journal entries:

- Weather conditions and moon phases

- Sleep quality rating

- Physical sensations upon waking

- Dominant colors or visual elements

- Key emotions and their intensity

- Recurring symbols or themes

- Questions or insights that arise

Some find success with bullet-point formatting for quick morning capture:

- Main dream events

- Key characters

- Setting details

- Emotional highlights

- Unusual elements

- Physical sensations

- Lingering questions

The key is finding a format that you can maintain consistently while half-awake, then expanding on later when fully alert. Start simple and adjust your approach based on what yields the most meaningful insights for your personal dream exploration journey.

The crucial moments for dream journaling occur in those hazy first seconds of waking. Like morning dew evaporating in sunlight, dream memories fade rapidly once consciousness takes hold. Keep your journal and pen within arm's reach of your bed - even a few seconds of movement can scatter those precious dream fragments.

Don't worry about complete sentences or proper grammar in these early morning captures. Quick bullet points or rough sketches work perfectly. The goal is getting the essence down before it slips away. Even seemingly nonsensical fragments like "blue door" or "falling leaves" can later trigger fuller dream recall.

Some find success recording dreams multiple times throughout the night. Setting a gentle alarm during natural wake periods (typically every 90 minutes during REM cycles) allows capture of dreams from different sleep stages. However, this approach requires balancing dream documentation against sleep quality.

For those who wake naturally during the night, keeping a small book light or dim bedside lamp helps minimize disruption. Voice recorders offer an eyes-closed alternative, though some find speaking aloud too jarring for maintaining that delicate half-awake state where dreams linger.

Morning journaling works best before checking phones or starting daily routines. The mind remains closer to the dream state before engaging with external stimuli. Even brief exposure to news, social media, or work emails can override fragile dream memories with new information.

When recording dreams feels challenging, start with simple emotional notes - was the dream pleasant, frightening, confusing? These emotional anchors often help retrieve associated dream content later. Physical sensations also provide useful memory triggers.

Beyond basic dream recording, deeper analysis requires a systematic approach to uncover patterns and meanings. Consider these essential prompts when exploring your dreams:

- Emotions serve as powerful anchors for dream interpretation. Note both dominant feelings and subtle undertones - was there an underlying anxiety beneath surface excitement? Did emotions shift throughout the dream? Track how dream emotions compare to waking life moods. A persistent dream fear might signal unaddressed real-world concerns.

- Examine the dream setting in detail. Was it familiar or foreign? Indoor or outdoor? Dark or light? Natural or urban? Settings often reflect our psychological landscape. A cramped room could represent feeling trapped, while open meadows might suggest freedom or possibility.

- Pay attention to dream characters. Who appeared? How did they interact with you? Were they known to you or strangers? Dream figures frequently embody aspects of ourselves or represent relationships needing attention. A recurring authority figure might highlight issues with power or control.

- Color holds significance in dreams. Note prominent colors and their associations. Red often connects to passion or anger, while blue may represent tranquility or depression. Personal and cultural associations matter - your unique history shapes how colors speak to you.

- Record any numbers, words, or messages that appeared. Even seemingly random sequences might reveal patterns over time. A repeated number could point to significant dates or quantities in your life.

- Movement patterns offer insights. Were you running, flying, falling, or stuck? Physical sensations in dreams often mirror emotional states. Falling might indicate loss of control, while flying could represent liberation or escape.

- Note your role in the dream. Were you an active participant or passive observer? Did you feel powerful or powerless? Your dream position often reflects how you view yourself in waking life.

These analytical prompts help transform scattered dream fragments into meaningful insights about your inner world. Regular practice reveals personal symbols and themes unique to your dreamscape.

Reviewing your dream journal reveals patterns that might otherwise remain hidden. Weekly analysis helps identify recurring symbols, themes, and emotional states that surface in your dreams. Start by highlighting common elements - specific objects, people, or situations that appear multiple times. Create categories like "water dreams" or "chase sequences" to organize similar experiences.

Monthly reviews provide a broader perspective. Mark significant life events alongside dream entries to spot correlations. Did work stress coincide with dreams of being unprepared? Did relationship changes trigger dreams of old homes? These connections often become apparent only through systematic review.

Color-coding helps track different dream elements. Use highlighters to mark emotions in yellow, locations in blue, and significant symbols in green. This visual system makes patterns jump out when scanning multiple entries. Create a simple tally system to count how often specific symbols or themes appear.

Consider creating a dream timeline. Plot major dream themes against real-world events on a calendar or spreadsheet. This helps identify potential triggers and patterns in your dream cycle. Note how themes shift with seasons, work cycles, or personal milestones.

Cross-referencing reveals subtle connections between dreams and daily life. Did that recurring dream of losing teeth start when you began questioning your career path? Does flying show up more often during periods of personal freedom? Keep a separate section in your journal for these observations.

Develop a symbol key specific to your dreams. While traditional dream dictionaries offer general interpretations, your personal associations matter more. That black cat might represent bad luck in folklore, but perhaps it reminds you of a childhood pet who brought comfort. Track how your relationship with specific symbols evolves over time.

Look for emotional patterns rather than just literal repetitions. Dreams about different situations might share underlying feelings of vulnerability or empowerment. Group dreams by emotional theme to understand what feelings demand attention in your waking life.

11

Creating a Dream-Friendly Sleep Environment

C reating the perfect sleep environment significantly impacts both sleep quality and dream recall. A room that's too warm or too cold can disrupt the natural sleep cycle, affecting the crucial REM periods where most vivid dreams occur. The ideal bedroom temperature ranges between 60-67°F (15-19°C), allowing the body's core temperature to naturally decrease during sleep onset.

Darkness proves essential for maintaining proper circadian rhythms. Even small amounts of light can interfere with melatonin production, the hormone responsible for regulating sleep-wake cycles. Blackout curtains effectively block street lights, early morning sun, and other environmental light sources that might otherwise fragment sleep patterns and interrupt dreams. For optimal results, eliminate all sources of artificial light, including LED displays from electronics and charging devices.

Sound control plays an equally vital role. While complete silence works for some, others benefit from consistent background noise to mask disruptive sounds. White noise machines offer a steady stream of sound that helps maintain sleep continuity without jarring interruptions that could pull you out of dream states. The consistent audio frequency helps mask sudden changes in environmental noise that might otherwise trigger wake responses.

The combination of proper temperature, complete darkness, and controlled sound creates an optimal sleep sanctuary. This environmental foundation supports the brain's natural transition through sleep cycles, particularly during REM periods when dreams are most likely to occur and be remembered. Consider these elements as tools in your dream exploration toolkit - each one contributing to the likelihood of experiencing and recalling meaningful dreams.

A sleep environment audit can reveal areas for improvement. Check for light leaks around windows, monitor room temperature throughout the night, and assess noise levels during different times. Small adjustments often yield significant improvements in both sleep quality and dream recall ability.

For those living in urban environments, additional considerations might include soundproofing windows or using heavy curtains that serve both light-blocking and sound-dampening purposes. The goal is to create a consistent, controlled environment that supports undisturbed sleep cycles and enhances dream experiences.

The transition from waking life to sleep benefits greatly from intentional evening rituals. Just as ancient cultures developed ceremonies to honor the dream state, modern sleep preparation can incorporate meaningful practices that prime both body and mind for enhanced dream experiences.

Aromatherapy offers a powerful tool for creating this transition. Lavender, with its scientifically proven calming properties, reduces anxiety and promotes deeper sleep when diffused in the bedroom. The scent molecules interact with the limbic system, triggering relaxation responses that ease the mind into a more receptive state for dreaming. Other beneficial essential oils include chamomile, vanilla, and cedarwood, each contributing unique properties to support restful sleep.

Sound plays a crucial role in preparing for dream-rich sleep. Soft instrumental music between 60-80 beats per minute mirrors the heart's resting rhythm, naturally slowing breathing patterns and calming the nervous system. Guided meditations specifically designed for sleep incorporate techniques like progressive muscle relaxation and visualization, helping to release physical tension that might otherwise interrupt dream cycles.

These pre-sleep rituals work best when performed consistently, training the brain to recognize these sensory cues as signals to begin the transition toward sleep. The key lies in selecting practices that resonate personally and can be maintained regularly. Simple actions like dimming lights, sipping caffeine-free tea, or gentle stretching can become powerful sleep triggers when performed mindfully each evening.

The effectiveness of these routines stems from their ability to create clear boundaries between daytime activity and nighttime rest. This separation helps quiet the analytical mind that often interferes with dream recall, allowing easier access to the subconscious during sleep. When combined with proper environmental conditions, these practices establish an optimal foundation for vivid dreaming and subsequent memory retention.

Sleep disruptions can significantly impact our ability to remember dreams, particularly when they interrupt crucial REM cycles. A sleep mask serves as more than just a barrier against light - it creates a consistent darkness that supports the production of melatonin, our body's natural sleep hormone. The gentle pressure around the eyes also provides a subtle reminder not to open them when briefly stirring during the night, helping maintain that delicate bridge between sleep and wakefulness where dreams often linger.

Quality sleep masks should be made of breathable, natural materials like silk or cotton to prevent skin irritation and overheating. The best designs feature adjustable straps that won't tangle in hair or slip during movement, and molded eye cups that prevent pressure on the eyelids while blocking out all ambient light.

A consistent sleep schedule works hand-in-hand with these tools by aligning our internal circadian rhythms. The body operates on a 24-hour cycle, and

REM sleep tends to be most profound during the early morning hours. By maintaining regular sleep and wake times - even on weekends - we strengthen these natural patterns. This consistency helps optimize the timing and duration of REM cycles, when most vivid dreams occur.

Research shows that adults need between 7-9 hours of sleep per night to cycle through all sleep stages properly. Going to bed and waking at the same times helps regulate body temperature, hormone production, and other biological processes that influence sleep quality. Even small variations of 30-60 minutes can disrupt these patterns.

Electronic devices pose a particular challenge to maintaining sleep consistency. The blue light emitted by phones, tablets, and computers suppresses melatonin production. Setting a "digital sunset" - turning off devices 1-2 hours before bedtime - helps the brain transition naturally into sleep mode. Using apps that automatically adjust screen color temperature to warmer tones in the evening can help when complete avoidance isn't practical.

White noise machines or fans can mask irregular sounds that might otherwise interrupt sleep cycles. The steady background noise creates an acoustic barrier against sudden disturbances like traffic, household noises, or neighbors.

The foods and beverages we consume in the hours before sleep can dramatically influence our dream experiences and ability to remember them. Caffeine, found not just in coffee but also in chocolate, tea, and many sodas, can disrupt sleep patterns up to six hours after consumption. Even small amounts can prevent the brain from entering deeper sleep stages where vivid dreams occur.

Heavy meals close to bedtime force the body to focus on digestion rather than optimal sleep. The energy diverted to processing food can raise body temperature and cause discomfort, leading to fragmented sleep and interrupted dream cycles. Spicy or acidic foods may trigger indigestion or reflux, creating physical discomfort that pulls us out of dream states.

Staying properly hydrated supports brain function and dream recall, but timing is crucial. Dehydration can cause headaches and grogginess that make it harder to remember dreams upon waking. However, drinking too much water before bed leads to midnight bathroom trips that interrupt valuable REM sleep.

The key is maintaining steady hydration throughout the day and tapering off liquid intake in the evening hours.

Certain nutrients may enhance dream activity and recall. Foods rich in B6, like bananas, avocados, and whole grains, help the body produce serotonin which influences sleep quality and dreaming. Tryptophan-containing foods such as turkey, nuts, and seeds provide building blocks for melatonin production.

The ideal approach is eating a light, balanced dinner at least three hours before bedtime. If hunger strikes later, small protein-rich snacks like a handful of almonds or a small piece of cheese can prevent blood sugar drops that might disturb sleep. Herbal teas like chamomile or valerian root can promote relaxation without the stimulating effects of caffeine.

For optimal dream recall, consider keeping a glass of water on the nightstand. Taking small sips when needed prevents the disruption of getting up, while maintaining the hydration necessary for mental clarity upon waking. This practice supports the delicate transition between sleep and wakefulness when dreams are most easily remembered.

12

Mindfulness Practices to Enhance Recall

M indfulness creates a bridge between your waking and dreaming consciousness. By cultivating present-moment awareness during the day, you strengthen your ability to notice and remember dreams. The practice of observing thoughts without judgment carries over into sleep, making dream recall more natural and effortless.

Simple mindfulness exercises prepare your mind for better dream retention. Take five minutes each morning to scan your body from head to toe, noting physical sensations. This trains your awareness to pick up subtle details that often slip away when remembering dreams. Practice following your breath throughout the day, anchoring yourself to the present moment.

Walking meditation offers another pathway to heightened dream awareness. Move slowly and deliberately, feeling each foot connect with the ground. Notice the shifting of weight, the swing of your arms, the rhythm of your breath. This careful attention to physical movement helps you recognize similar sensations within dreams.

During daily activities, pause periodically to take in your surroundings with all senses. Notice the play of light on surfaces, ambient sounds, textures against your skin, subtle scents in the air. This multi-sensory awareness strengthens your ability to recall vivid dream details.

Set mindful intentions before sleep by taking three conscious breaths. On the inhale, silently say "I am aware." On the exhale, release tension and mental chatter. This creates a receptive state for dream experiences and memories.

Keep your attention on physical sensations as you drift toward sleep. Notice the weight of your body on the mattress, the temperature of the air, the rhythm of your heartbeat. This present-moment awareness often carries into the dream state, making memories more accessible upon waking.

Practice the "STOP" technique throughout your day - Stop, Take a breath, Observe your surroundings, Proceed mindfully. This trains your mind to pause and notice details that might otherwise go unregistered, whether awake or dreaming.

Pre-sleep mindfulness exercises create optimal conditions for dream recall and vivid dreaming experiences. By clearing mental clutter and setting focused intentions, you prepare your consciousness for deeper dream engagement.

The body scan meditation offers a systematic approach to releasing physical and mental tension before sleep. Start by lying comfortably on your back, arms at your sides with palms facing up. Bring attention to your toes, noticing any sensations without trying to change them. Gradually move awareness up through your feet, ankles, and legs. Notice areas of tightness or discomfort without judgment. Continue scanning upward through your hips, lower back, and abdomen. Feel the gentle rise and fall of your breath. Progress through your chest, shoulders, and arms down to your fingertips. Finally, bring awareness to your neck, face, and scalp. This practice typically takes 10-15 minutes and naturally induces a state of relaxed alertness conducive to dream recall.

Simple breathing exercises effectively calm an active mind before sleep. The 4-7-8 breath pattern particularly helps transition from daily concerns to a receptive dream state. Inhale quietly through your nose for a count of four. Hold the breath for a count of seven. Exhale completely through your mouth for a count of eight, making a whoosh sound. This cycle reduces anxiety and mental chatter that can interfere with dream memory.

Another effective technique is alternate nostril breathing. Using your right thumb, close your right nostril and inhale slowly through the left. At the peak of inhalation, close the left nostril with your ring finger while releasing the thumb and exhaling through the right nostril. Inhale through the right nostril, then close it. Release the ring finger and exhale through the left nostril. This balanced breathing pattern harmonizes both brain hemispheres, creating ideal conditions for vivid dreaming.

Square breathing offers another option, especially helpful for analytical minds. Visualize tracing a square as you breathe - inhale for four counts up one side, hold for four counts across the top, exhale for four counts down the other side, hold empty for four counts across the bottom. This geometric pattern gives the mind a simple focus while deepening relaxation.

Regular mindfulness practice strengthens the connection between waking awareness and dream consciousness, enhancing both dream recall and the potential for lucid dreaming. By cultivating present-moment awareness during daily activities, you develop the mental muscles needed to recognize when you're dreaming.

Reality checks serve as powerful tools for developing this heightened awareness. Throughout the day, pause to question whether you're dreaming. Common checks include trying to push your finger through your palm, looking at text or digital displays twice to see if they change, or attempting to float. The key lies not in the specific action but in the genuine questioning of reality. When these checks become habit, they often carry over into dreams, triggering lucidity.

Physical reality checks work best when paired with mindful observation of your surroundings. Notice the quality of light, the behavior of shadows, and the logic of events unfolding around you. Dreams often contain subtle inconsistencies - lights that don't cast proper shadows, digital clocks showing impossible times, or physics behaving unusually. Training yourself to notice these details while awake increases your chances of spotting them while dreaming.

Dream signs - recurring themes, objects, or situations that frequently appear in your dreams - become more apparent through mindful awareness. These personal markers might include flying, meeting deceased relatives, or finding yourself in familiar locations from your past. By maintaining awareness of your common dream signs during waking hours, you create mental triggers that can spark lucidity when encountered in dreams.

The practice of "mindful gaps" throughout the day enhances dream awareness. These brief pauses involve stopping whatever you're doing to take three conscious breaths while fully experiencing your surroundings. This trains the mind to move from automatic pilot to conscious awareness - a crucial skill for recognizing the dream state.

Combining these practices with regular meditation strengthens the mind's ability to maintain awareness during sleep transitions. Even short sessions of focused breathing or body awareness can improve dream recall and increase chances of achieving lucidity. The key lies in consistency rather than duration - five minutes of daily practice proves more effective than occasional longer sessions.

Integrating mindfulness into daily life doesn't require drastic changes or hours of meditation. Small, consistent practices create lasting habits that enhance dream awareness and recall. Setting phone reminders at regular intervals - perhaps every two hours - prompts brief moments of conscious awareness. These micro-breaks serve as opportunities to check in with your senses, notice your surroundings, and ground yourself in the present moment.

Morning commutes offer natural opportunities for mindfulness practice. Instead of automatically scrolling through social media, use red lights or train stops as triggers to observe your breath and body sensations. Notice the temperature, the sounds around you, and the quality of light. This heightened awareness carries over into dream recall, as the mind becomes more attuned to subtle details.

Meal times present another anchor point for mindful awareness. Before eating, pause to observe the colors, textures, and aromas of your food. This simple practice strengthens the neural pathways responsible for sensory awareness, which proves valuable when recalling dream details.

Evening routines benefit particularly from grounding exercises. A three-minute body scan while lying in bed helps transition from day to night. Start at your toes, gradually moving attention upward through each body part, releasing tension and noting physical sensations. This practice calms the nervous system and creates optimal conditions for dream recall.

Simple environmental cues can trigger mindful moments throughout the day. Place small objects - perhaps a smooth stone or meaningful trinket - in frequently visited locations. When you notice these objects, use them as reminders to take three conscious breaths and check in with your current experience.

Bedtime grounding exercises might include gentle stretching focused on connecting with the earth. Standing barefoot, feel the pressure and texture beneath your feet. Roll slowly from heel to toe, awakening sensory awareness in your feet and ankles. This physical grounding translates into more stable dream recall, as it strengthens the mind-body connection essential for remembering dreams.

These practices work best when tailored to your natural daily rhythms. Choose anchor points that align with your existing routine rather than forcing new habits that feel unnatural or burdensome.

13

Spiritual Messages in Dreams

Throughout history, cultures worldwide have viewed dreams as sacred channels of communication between the earthly and divine realms. Ancient texts overflow with accounts of divine messages delivered through dreams, offering guidance, warnings, and prophecies to those deemed worthy of receiving them.

The Bible contains numerous examples of prophetic dreams. Joseph's dreams in Genesis foretold his rise to power in Egypt, while Daniel's ability to interpret Nebuchadnezzar's dreams elevated him to a position of influence. In the New Testament, an angel appears to Joseph in a dream, warning him to flee to Egypt with Mary and Jesus to escape Herod's persecution.

Native American traditions hold dreams in particularly high regard, viewing them as direct communications from spirit guides and ancestors. The Iroquois believe that dreams reveal one's deepest desires and needs, requiring community attention and interpretation. During their traditional midwinter ceremony, tribal members share significant dreams and perform rituals to honor these nocturnal messages.

Australian Aboriginal peoples maintain a profound connection to the Dreamtime - a spiritual dimension where past, present, and future converge. Their tradition teaches that dreams provide access to this sacred realm, allowing communion with ancestral spirits who share wisdom and maintain cultural continuity.

In Buddhist philosophy, dreams serve as bridges to higher states of consciousness. Tibetan Dream Yoga practitioners cultivate awareness within dreams to achieve spiritual enlightenment, viewing the dream state as an opportunity to transcend ordinary perception and connect with divine wisdom.

Ancient Egyptians constructed special sleep temples where seekers would rest, hoping to receive healing messages from the gods through their dreams. Priests would interpret these divine communications, prescribing treatments or offering guidance based on the symbolic content revealed.

The Islamic tradition acknowledges different categories of dreams, with the most significant being "true dreams" or ruya, believed to come from Allah. Prophet Muhammad's divine revelations often came through dreams, establishing a precedent for dreams as vehicles of spiritual truth in Islamic mysticism.

These diverse spiritual traditions share a common thread - recognizing dreams as portals through which divine wisdom flows into human consciousness. While modern science offers neurological explanations for dreaming, many continue to find profound spiritual significance in their nocturnal visions.

Across cultures and belief systems, certain dream symbols consistently emerge as bearers of spiritual significance. These universal symbols often transcend cultural boundaries, appearing in dreams worldwide with remarkably similar interpretations.

Angels frequently manifest in dreams as luminous beings radiating peace and protection. They might appear with traditional features - wings, halos, or flowing robes - or simply as intense points of light. Their presence often coincides with periods of personal struggle or important life transitions, offering comfort and divine guidance. Some dreamers report angels appearing during times of grief or loss, bringing messages of hope and reassurance.

Light in dreams carries profound spiritual symbolism. A sudden burst of brightness might illuminate a darkened dreamscape, representing a moment of spiritual awakening or divine insight. Golden light often signals spiritual wisdom or enlightenment, while pure white light typically represents divine presence or unconditional love. Dreams of walking toward light or being enveloped by it frequently precede major spiritual breakthroughs or life changes.

Spiritual light in dreams takes various forms - a distant star guiding the way, a doorway filled with radiance, or a gentle glow emanating from within objects or beings. The quality of this light differs from ordinary dream imagery, often described as more vivid and accompanied by feelings of peace, clarity, or profound understanding.

The intensity of these spiritual symbols often correlates with their significance. A faint angelic presence might suggest subtle guidance, while an overwhelming light experience could indicate a major spiritual awakening or divine intervention. The context matters - angels appearing in dreams during decision-making periods often point toward specific choices or paths, while light experiences tend to represent broader spiritual transformations or revelations.

These symbols resonate particularly strongly with individuals going through personal crises or spiritual seeking phases, offering guidance when conventional wisdom falls short. Their appearance in dreams often marks significant turning points in one's spiritual journey, serving as waypoints or confirmations of spiritual growth.

Intuition serves as a vital bridge between the conscious mind and spiritual dream messages. Unlike logical analysis, intuitive understanding flows naturally, offering immediate insights without conscious reasoning. This innate knowing often manifests as a gut feeling or sudden clarity about a dream's meaning.

During spiritual dreams, intuition acts as an internal compass, helping dreamers navigate complex symbolic landscapes. A dreamer might encounter abstract symbols or scenarios that defy logical interpretation, yet intuitively grasp their personal significance. This understanding frequently arrives as an instantaneous knowing rather than through step-by-step analysis.

Meditation enhances this intuitive connection. By practicing regular meditation, dreamers develop heightened awareness of subtle energies and meanings within their dreams. Simple breathing exercises before sleep create mental space for intuitive insights to surface. Even five minutes of focused breathing can strengthen the bridge between conscious awareness and spiritual understanding.

Prayer offers another pathway to intuitive dream interpretation. Whether formal or conversational, prayer creates a receptive state where spiritual messages become clearer. Many find success with a practice of evening prayer followed by dream journaling upon waking, allowing intuitive insights to flow naturally onto the page.

The effectiveness of these practices increases with consistency. Regular meditation builds neural pathways that support intuitive processing, while ongoing prayer practice deepens spiritual receptivity. These tools work best when approached without rigid expectations, allowing natural intuitive abilities to unfold gradually.

The path to developing dream intuition begins with simple yet powerful practices. These exercises require no special knowledge or equipment - only dedication and an open mind. By incorporating them into your daily routine, you strengthen the natural connection between conscious awareness and dream insights.

Sitting in silence before bed creates mental space for dream messages to emerge. Find a comfortable position, dim the lights, and allow your thoughts to settle. This isn't meditation - there's no need to clear your mind completely. Simply observe your thoughts without judgment as they drift past. The quiet moments prime your brain for more vivid dream recall.

Upon waking, pause before reaching for your phone or starting your day. Notice your first emotional responses - a lingering sense of peace, traces of anxiety, or perhaps a feeling of wonder. These immediate impressions often carry important dream messages before the logical mind begins analyzing them.

Physical sensations provide another window into dream meaning. While reflecting on a dream, pay attention to subtle body signals - a tightness in your chest, butterflies in your stomach, or a sensation of lightness. Your body often recognizes dream significance before your conscious mind catches up.

A dream symbol journal differs from traditional dream journaling. Rather than attempting to interpret symbols, simply record them without analysis. Note recurring images, colors, numbers, or themes. Over time, patterns emerge naturally without forced interpretation.

Creating quiet space each morning allows intuitive insights to surface organically. Before jumping into daily activities, spend a few minutes in receptive silence. Dreams often reveal their meaning gradually when given space to unfold. This gentle approach yields deeper understanding than aggressive analysis.

These practices work best when approached consistently but without pressure. There's no need to master them all at once. Start with one that resonates and gradually incorporate others. The key lies in patient, regular practice rather than seeking immediate results.

Ancient cultures understood the power of ritual in accessing spiritual wisdom through dreams. By creating sacred space before sleep, modern dreamers can tap into this timeless practice of dream incubation - the art of intentionally seeking guidance through dreams.

Dream incubation begins with preparing your sleeping environment. Remove electronic devices and clutter that might disrupt spiritual energy. Writing your intention before sleep strengthens the dream incubation process. Use a dedicated journal to record specific questions or areas where you seek guidance. Rather than demanding answers, frame your writing as an open invitation for wisdom to come through your dreams.

A purifying bath with sea salt cleanses both body and energy field, washing away the day's mental clutter. The warm water relaxes tense muscles while the salt's minerals draw out negativity, creating clarity for dream work.

Candlelight provides a focal point for setting intentions. The gentle flicker creates an atmosphere conducive to introspection. Place the candle safely away from flammable objects, allowing its warm glow to fill the room while writing intentions in a dream journal or sitting in contemplation.

Gentle stretching or yoga poses release physical tension that could disrupt sleep. Cat-cow poses flex the spine, while child's pose grounds energy. Forward folds calm the nervous system. These movements transition the body from daily activity into restfulness while maintaining awareness.

Meditation or prayer deepens the connection to spiritual guidance. Even 5-10 minutes of focused breathing creates mental stillness. Some find comfort in traditional prayers, while others prefer silent meditation. The key is consistency - establishing a regular practice signals readiness for spiritual insight.

Reading spiritual texts before sleep plants seeds in the subconscious mind. Ancient dream temples prescribed specific passages to inspire prophetic dreams. Modern practitioners might choose sacred texts, poetry, or inspirational writing that resonates with their path. The content matters less than the mindful act of engaging with wisdom literature.

These practices work best when customized to individual needs and beliefs. Some may prefer shorter rituals while others dedicate more time. The essential elements are creating sacred space, setting clear intention, and maintaining consistent practice. Over time, this dedication cultivates deeper connection between conscious and unconscious realms.

The timing of dream incubation matters. Many find success working with lunar cycles, particularly during the full moon when intuitive energies peak. Others align their practice with personally significant dates or religious observances.

Consistency strengthens the effectiveness of dream incubation. Choose rituals that resonate with your beliefs and lifestyle, then practice them regularly. Over time, these repeated actions create a powerful container for spiritual dream experiences.

Remember that dream guidance often arrives in unexpected forms. While some receive clear messages, others might experience subtle shifts in awareness or seemingly unrelated dreams that later reveal their significance. Trust that the wisdom comes in the form most beneficial for your growth.

14

Scientific Insights into Dream Interpretation

M odern neuroscience has revolutionized our understanding of dreams through advanced brain imaging techniques. During dream states, functional magnetic resonance imaging (fMRI) reveals intense activity in the visual cortex, explaining the vivid imagery dreamers experience. The amygdala and hippocampus light up simultaneously, processing emotions and memories that weave into dream narratives.

PET scans show increased blood flow to the anterior cingulate cortex during REM sleep, an area associated with conflict resolution and emotional processing. This activation suggests dreams play a crucial role in working through daily stresses and unresolved feelings.

EEG studies capture the distinct brain wave patterns of dreaming. Beta waves diminish as alpha waves take over, signaling the transition from wakefulness to early sleep stages. Theta waves dominate during active dreaming, their rhythmic patterns correlating with dream intensity and recall ability.

Large-scale psychological studies have identified universal dream themes across cultures. Research tracking thousands of dream reports reveals common patterns: falling, being chased, losing teeth, or appearing unprepared for an exam. These shared experiences suggest underlying psychological mechanisms that transcend cultural boundaries.

Statistical analysis of dream content shows correlations between daily activities and dream themes. Athletes frequently dream of physical performance, while students often dream about academic challenges. This "day residue" effect appears consistently in research data, supporting theories about dreams processing recent experiences.

Sleep labs document physiological responses during dreams. Heart rate variability, muscle tension, and eye movements provide measurable data about dream states. These biological markers help researchers identify when participants enter REM sleep and experience vivid dreams.

Brain imaging during lucid dreaming offers unique insights. When dreamers become aware they're dreaming, specific regions in the prefrontal cortex activate, suggesting conscious control over dream content. This finding opens new avenues for understanding consciousness and its relationship to dream states.

Population studies reveal age-related changes in dream patterns. Children report more fantastic elements, while adult dreams tend toward realistic scenarios. Elderly individuals often experience decreased dream recall, correlating with changes in sleep architecture and brain chemistry.

Scientific approaches to dream research offer both powerful insights and notable limitations. Brain imaging techniques like fMRI and PET scans excel at mapping neural activity during dreams, revealing consistent patterns across large populations. These tools identify which brain regions activate during specific dream experiences, providing concrete evidence of dream-related processes.

Statistical analysis proves particularly effective at uncovering universal dream themes. Large-scale studies across different countries and cultures consistently find shared experiences - falling dreams appear in roughly 75% of participants, while being chased occurs in over 80% of reported dreams. This data helps establish baseline patterns for understanding typical dream content.

Laboratory sleep studies contribute valuable quantitative data through physiological measurements. Heart rate, brain waves, and muscle activity during REM sleep create reproducible markers of dream states. These biological indicators help researchers track dream cycles and intensity with scientific precision.

However, scientific methods struggle to capture the deeply personal nature of dreams. While brain scans might show increased activity in the amygdala during an emotional dream, they cannot reveal the specific memories or cultural associations that make that dream meaningful to the individual. The same dream symbol - a snake, for instance - might represent healing to one person and danger to another, nuances that statistical analysis often misses.

Cultural context poses another challenge for scientific approaches. While research can identify common dream themes across populations, it often fails to account for how cultural beliefs and practices influence dream interpretation. Traditional scientific methods may overlook the significance of specific symbols or scenarios that hold deep meaning within particular communities.

The rigid framework of scientific methodology can also limit understanding of more subtle aspects of dreaming. Intuitive insights, spiritual experiences, and personal growth through dreams often defy quantitative measurement. These elements, while potentially significant to the dreamer, remain difficult to validate through conventional scientific means.

Additionally, laboratory settings may affect natural dream patterns. The presence of monitoring equipment and unfamiliar environments can alter sleep quality and dream content, potentially skewing research results. This "observer effect" highlights the challenge of studying dreams while maintaining authentic sleep conditions.

Scientific research has produced several compelling theories about why we dream, each supported by extensive studies and evidence. The activation-synthesis hypothesis, first proposed by psychiatrists J. Allan Hobson and Robert McCarley in 1977, suggests dreams result from our brain's attempt to create coherent stories from random neural firing during REM sleep.

According to this theory, the brain stem generates electrical signals that activate various brain regions responsible for emotions, sensations, and memories.

As these signals fire randomly, our frontal cortex works to synthesize this neural activity into a narrative that makes sense to us. This explains why dreams often contain bizarre elements - our brain is simply doing its best to interpret random neural impulses.

Brain imaging studies support this hypothesis by showing increased activity in emotional and memory centers during REM sleep, while the logical, reasoning parts of our brain show reduced activity. This combination creates the perfect environment for our minds to generate unusual scenarios without questioning their logic.

The threat simulation theory, developed by Finnish psychologist Antti Revonsuo, takes an evolutionary approach. This theory proposes that dreams serve as a biological defense mechanism, allowing us to safely practice responding to threatening situations. Like a flight simulator for pilots, our dreams create virtual reality scenarios where we can rehearse survival skills without real danger.

Research backing this theory shows that approximately 70% of dreams contain some form of threat or conflict situation. These threats often reflect ancient survival challenges - being chased, falling, or confronting hostile entities. Even in modern society, where physical threats are less common, our dreams continue to simulate threatening scenarios that help us practice emotional and social survival skills.

The threat simulation theory also explains why negative emotions appear more frequently in dreams than positive ones. Studies indicate that anxiety, fear, and aggression occur more often in dreams than joy or contentment, suggesting dreams prioritize preparing us for challenging situations over pleasant experiences.

Both theories demonstrate how dreams serve vital biological and psychological functions, moving beyond older views of dreams as merely random mental activity or symbolic messages.

Recent advances in dream research have revolutionized our understanding of the dreaming mind, particularly through artificial intelligence applications. Machine learning algorithms now analyze thousands of dream reports simultaneously, identifying patterns and connections that human researchers might miss. These AI systems detect recurring themes, emotional content, and symbolic associations across diverse populations.

Neural networks trained on extensive dream databases can predict common dream elements based on demographic data, stress levels, and daily activities. This predictive capability helps researchers understand how external factors influence dream content. For instance, AI analysis revealed that people living in urban environments often dream of nature scenes, possibly reflecting an innate need for connection with the natural world.

AI-powered natural language processing examines the linguistic patterns in dream reports, uncovering subtle relationships between word choice and emotional states. These systems have identified that anxious individuals tend to use more motion-related words in their dream descriptions, while depressed individuals often employ static or passive language.

Computer vision algorithms now map the visual elements of dreams described in reports, creating digital representations that help researchers understand spatial and temporal patterns in dream narratives. This technology has shown that dreams often follow similar structural patterns across cultures, suggesting universal elements in human dream experiences.

Deep learning models have begun identifying correlations between dream content and various health conditions, opening new possibilities for early detection of psychological and neurological disorders. These systems can spot subtle changes in dream patterns that might indicate the onset of conditions like anxiety disorders or depression before traditional symptoms appear.

The integration of AI with traditional sleep monitoring equipment has enhanced our ability to track brain activity patterns during dreams. Advanced algorithms can now predict with increasing accuracy when a person is dreaming and even make educated guesses about the dream's emotional tone based on neural activity patterns.

These technological developments have transformed dream research from a largely subjective field into one backed by data-driven insights, while still respecting the deeply personal nature of individual dream experiences.

15

Harmonizing Spiritual and Empirical Views

T he integration of scientific and spiritual perspectives on dreams presents one of the most challenging aspects of dream research. While science seeks measurable, repeatable patterns through brain wave analysis and neurochemical studies, spiritual interpretations focus on the ineffable - personal meaning, divine messages, and soul connections that defy quantification.

This tension becomes particularly evident when examining how dreams influence decision-making. Scientific models suggest dreams emerge from neural processing, with brain activity following deterministic patterns based on previous experiences and biological needs. These models view dreams as products of complex but ultimately predictable neurological systems, much like a sophisticated computer processing data during downtime.

Yet this mechanistic view conflicts with spiritual frameworks that see dreams as channels for free will, divine guidance, and personal transformation. When someone dreams of taking a new career path, science might attribute this to subconscious processing of career dissatisfaction, while spiritual interpretations could view it as divine guidance or the soul's deeper wisdom emerging.

The conflict extends to dream symbols and their meanings. Scientific approaches analyze symbols through psychological and cultural lenses, seeking statistical patterns and correlations. A snake in a dream might be linked to evolutionary fear responses or cultural conditioning. Spiritual traditions, however, might interpret the same snake as a sacred messenger or representation of kundalini energy, meanings that transcend material explanation.

Brain imaging studies can show increased activity in emotion-processing regions during nightmares, but they cannot capture the profound sense of spiritual insight many people report from challenging dreams. Similarly, while sleep labs can measure REM cycles with precision, they cannot quantify the feeling of receiving wisdom from an ancestral figure in a dream.

This disconnect creates a practical challenge for dream interpretation. Should someone experiencing recurring dreams of flight prioritize the neurological explanation of altered spatial processing during REM sleep, or explore the spiritual symbolism of transcendence and freedom? The scientific evidence supports both perspectives - dreams serve biological functions while also carrying profound personal meaning that extends beyond measurable parameters.

Carl Jung's groundbreaking work offers one of the most successful integrations of scientific and spiritual approaches to dream analysis. His analytical psychology framework bridges the gap between empirical observation and mystical insight, demonstrating how these perspectives can complement rather than contradict each other.

Jung's concept of the collective unconscious exemplifies this synthesis. Through careful documentation of dream patterns across cultures and time periods, he established scientific evidence for universal archetypal symbols. Yet he simultaneously honored the spiritual significance of these archetypes, recognizing them as conduits to deeper wisdom and personal transformation.

His work with mandalas illustrates this dual approach. Jung meticulously recorded and analyzed mandala symbols appearing in patients' dreams, documenting their geometric patterns and psychological effects with scientific rigor. At the same time, he acknowledged their sacred nature, noting how these circular designs reflected spiritual wholeness across religious traditions.

The Red Book represents another powerful example of Jung's integration. While maintaining detailed clinical notes and theoretical frameworks, he also embraced direct engagement with dream imagery through active imagination. This practice combined careful psychological observation with deep spiritual exploration, producing insights that informed both his scientific theories and understanding of the soul's journey.

Jung's analysis of alchemical symbols in dreams further demonstrates this synthesis. He approached alchemy both as a historical-psychological phenomenon worthy of scientific study and as a spiritual metaphor for personal transformation. By examining how alchemical symbols appeared in modern dreams, he showed how ancient spiritual wisdom could be understood through contemporary psychological frameworks.

His work with synchronicity - meaningful coincidences between dreams and external events - particularly challenged the divide between scientific and spiritual perspectives. Rather than dismissing these connections as mere superstition, Jung developed theoretical frameworks that could accommodate both causality and acausal relationships, expanding scientific understanding while preserving the mystery inherent in spiritual experience.

Understanding dreams requires a balanced approach that honors both scientific evidence and personal meaning-making. The biopsychosocial-spiritual model offers a comprehensive framework for interpreting dreams while respecting multiple perspectives.

At the biological level, this model examines how brain chemistry, sleep cycles, and neurological processes shape our dreams. REM sleep patterns, hormone fluctuations, and neural activation create the foundation for dream experiences. Consider how stress hormones like cortisol influence nightmare frequency, or how melatonin levels affect dream vividness.

The psychological component explores how our thoughts, emotions, and experiences manifest in dreams. Past trauma, daily stressors, and unconscious desires weave through our dreamscapes. A recurring dream about being unprepared for an exam might reflect work-related anxiety rather than literal academic concerns.

Social factors acknowledge how cultural background, relationships, and societal pressures impact dream content and interpretation. A snake in a dream might represent danger in Western cultures but wisdom in certain Eastern traditions. Family dynamics, social status, and cultural beliefs all filter into our dream experiences.

The biopsychosocial-spiritual model provides a comprehensive framework that honors both scientific evidence and personal meaning-making. This approach recognizes that dreams operate on multiple levels simultaneously, each offering valuable insights into our unconscious mind.

Consider a common dream of flying through the air. From a biological perspective, this sensation often correlates with the physical experience of REM sleep, where our bodies experience natural muscle paralysis and weightlessness. The same dream viewed through a psychological lens reveals our innate desires for freedom, independence, or escape from current limitations. Socially, flying dreams often reflect cultural narratives about power, success, and transcending ordinary boundaries. The spiritual dimension might interpret this as an expression of the soul's desire to connect with something greater than ourselves.

This integration of perspectives allows us to appreciate dreams' full complexity without dismissing any single aspect. Rather than forcing a choice between scientific explanation and personal meaning, this approach recognizes how these elements work together to create our dream experiences.

For those seeking to understand their dreams, this balanced framework offers multiple entry points for exploration. Whether you're drawn to the neurological mechanics of REM sleep, the psychological symbolism of dream imagery, or the potential spiritual significance of your dream experiences, each perspective contributes valuable insights to the whole.

Through this lens, we can examine dreams with both analytical rigor and open-minded curiosity, understanding that different aspects of dream interpretation may resonate more strongly at different times or for different individuals.

By examining dreams through these multiple lenses, we avoid reductionist interpretations while maintaining analytical clarity. This framework allows dreamers to find personal meaning while understanding the physiological and social contexts shaping their experiences.

To fully engage with your dreams, several practical tools prove invaluable. Sleep tracking apps and devices help identify your unique biological patterns, showing how your sleep cycles correspond to vivid dream periods and optimal recall times. By monitoring factors like sleep duration, movement, and environmental conditions, you'll recognize how physical elements influence your dream experiences.

A dream journal serves as your psychological compass, capturing raw dream content before it fades. Beyond simple recording, journaling reveals recurring themes, emotional patterns, and personal symbols that emerge over time. Through consistent documentation, you'll develop deeper awareness of how daily experiences and psychological states manifest in your dreams.

Understanding cultural context enriches dream interpretation by revealing how societal beliefs and shared symbols influence dream content. Research into different cultural perspectives on common dream themes - like falling, flying, or being chased - provides fresh insights into your own dream experiences. This broader awareness helps distinguish between universal dream patterns and culturally-specific meanings.

Meditation and contemplative practices create space for deeper dream exploration. Regular mindfulness exercises enhance dream recall and awareness while providing tools to process dream-related emotions and insights. These practices bridge the gap between conscious analysis and intuitive understanding, allowing for more nuanced dream interpretation.

Through combining these approaches - biological monitoring, psychological reflection, cultural awareness, and contemplative practice - you develop a more complete understanding of your dream life. This integrated toolkit honors both the scientific and personal dimensions of dreaming while providing practical methods for ongoing exploration.

Understanding your dreams requires developing a personalized approach that aligns with your beliefs, experiences, and comfort level with both scientific and spiritual perspectives. Like assembling a toolbox, you'll want to gather various interpretation methods that resonate with you while remaining open to new insights.

Before diving into dream interpretation techniques, it's essential to understand your own perspective on dreams. Your beliefs and experiences create a unique lens through which you view the dream world, influencing how you interpret and work with your dreams.

Take a moment to grab your journal. The following self-reflection questions will help illuminate your current relationship with dreams. There are no right or wrong answers - the goal is simply to bring awareness to your existing views and biases.

First, consider what you believe causes dreams. Do you view them primarily as random neural firing during sleep, meaningful messages from your subconscious, or perhaps communications from a higher power? Your answer reveals your baseline assumptions about dream origins.

Next, examine where you fall on the spectrum between scientific and spiritual explanations. Some people strongly prefer empirical evidence about brain chemistry and sleep cycles, while others resonate more with mystical or metaphysical interpretations. Most fall somewhere in between, finding value in both approaches.

Your cultural background and religious upbringing likely shape your dream perspective in subtle ways. Traditional beliefs passed down through your family or community may influence how you view certain dream symbols or experiences. Being aware of these inherited viewpoints helps you consciously choose which aspects to keep or modify.

Finally, reflect on powerful dream experiences that have impacted your beliefs. Perhaps you've had prophetic dreams that came true, recurring nightmares that resolved an emotional issue, or lucid dreams that expanded your sense of consciousness. These personal encounters often form the foundation of our dream philosophy.

Writing out your responses to these questions creates a snapshot of your current dream worldview. You can revisit these answers later to track how your perspective evolves as you learn new approaches to understanding your dreams.

Be honest about your biases. Perhaps you dismiss spiritual interpretations due to a scientific background, or maybe you struggle to accept neurological explanations because they feel too reductive. Acknowledging these biases helps you develop a more balanced approach.

Understanding dreams is a deeply personal journey, and your comfort level with different interpretation methods can significantly impact how effectively you work with your dreams. Before diving deeper into specific techniques, take a moment to assess your natural inclinations and potential resistance points.

Scientific analysis of brain patterns and sleep cycles offers concrete data about the mechanics of dreaming. Some find great comfort in understanding the neurological basis of dreams, with clear evidence from EEG readings and sleep studies providing a solid foundation for interpretation. Others may feel this approach strips dreams of their mystery and meaning.

Psychological examination brings attention to emotions and symbolic representations in dreams. This method bridges the gap between scientific rigor and personal meaning-making, appealing to those who appreciate structured analysis while honoring the subjective nature of dream experiences. The psychological approach often resonates with individuals who value self-reflection and emotional awareness.

Cultural and ancestral dream traditions carry wisdom passed down through generations. These approaches might feel deeply familiar if you grew up with specific cultural practices around dreaming, or they may seem foreign if you're exploring them for the first time. Consider how your cultural background influences your receptivity to traditional dream work.

Spiritual or religious interpretations view dreams as potential messages from a higher power or the divine. Your religious upbringing or current spiritual practice likely influences your openness to these perspectives. Some find profound meaning in spiritual dream interpretation, while others may feel skeptical or uncomfortable with supernatural explanations.

Personal intuition and felt sense rely on your inner knowing to understand dream messages. This approach requires trusting your instincts and immediate reactions to dream content. While some naturally gravitate toward intuitive interpretation, others may struggle to trust their inner guidance without external validation.

Take a moment to rate your comfort level with each of these approaches on a scale of 1-5. Your ratings reveal natural strengths and potential growth areas in your dream work. Remember, there's no obligation to use methods that feel fundamentally misaligned with your worldview.

Your comfort level with different interpretation methods shapes how effectively you engage with dream work, but expanding beyond familiar territory often yields the richest insights. Track your dream interpretations using multiple lenses.

Start by examining your ratings of various approaches. A high score for scientific methods might reflect confidence in analyzing sleep cycles, brain chemistry, and physiological factors affecting dreams. Meanwhile, lower scores for spiritual or intuitive approaches could indicate areas where gentle exploration might broaden your perspective. The goal isn't to abandon your strengths but to develop a more comprehensive understanding.

Create a dream journal that incorporates multiple viewpoints. Begin with concrete observations about your sleep environment, diet, and any medications that might influence dreaming. Note the room temperature, lighting conditions, and time you went to bed. These tangible factors provide a scientific foundation for understanding your dream experiences.

Next, record emotional patterns and life circumstances surrounding memorable dreams. Document any significant stressors, conflicts, or positive events that could influence dream content. This psychological layer helps reveal connections between waking life and dream symbols.

Consider cultural or ancestral wisdom that might illuminate dream meanings. If certain symbols appear repeatedly, research their significance across different traditions while remaining mindful of your personal and cultural context. This broader perspective can enrich your interpretation without requiring full adoption of any single viewpoint.

Finally, note practical insights or guidance received through dreams, whether they manifest as problem-solving breakthroughs, emotional resolution, or intuitive knowing. Track how these insights relate to your waking life decisions and personal growth. This practical application bridges the gap between different interpretation methods, showing how various approaches can work together to create meaningful understanding.

Remember that building a balanced practice takes time. Start with small steps in exploring unfamiliar approaches while maintaining your connection to methods that already serve you well. Over time, patterns will emerge showing which approaches yield the most meaningful insights for you. Remember, this is a personal journey - your interpretation style should evolve as you gain experience and understanding.

16

Dream Beliefs Across Cultures

Throughout human history, diverse cultures have developed unique perspectives on dreams, each offering profound insights into how different
societies understand these nocturnal experiences. These varied interpretations
reveal the universal human drive to find meaning in our dreams, while highlighting distinct cultural approaches to dream significance.

In many African traditions, dreams serve as a sacred bridge between the living
and their ancestors. The Xhosa people of South Africa believe dreams open
direct channels of communication with deceased family members who offer
guidance, warnings, and wisdom. During significant life transitions, such as
coming-of-age ceremonies or marriages, dreams hold particular importance as
ancestors may appear to bestow blessings or share vital teachings.

The Zulu culture treats dreams as messages from the amadlozi (ancestral spirits), requiring careful interpretation by skilled sangomas (traditional
healers). These practitioners help dreamers understand the symbolic language
through which ancestors speak, often involving animals, natural phenomena,
or departed relatives appearing in new forms.

For Aboriginal Australians, dreams connect to the concept of Dreamtime
or "The Dreaming" - a complex spiritual framework that describes both the

ancient past when ancestral beings created the world and an ongoing spiritual reality. Unlike Western views that often separate dreaming from waking life, Aboriginal cultures see dreams as extensions of reality where past, present, and future interconnect.

The Dreamtime encompasses creation stories where ancestral spirits shaped the landscape, established laws, and created all living things. Dreams serve as windows into this eternal spiritual dimension, allowing individuals to receive songs, stories, and knowledge passed down through generations. Aboriginal artists often draw inspiration from dreams, creating works that depict Dreamtime journeys and sacred narratives.

This intricate relationship between dreams and cultural identity demonstrates how dream interpretation varies significantly across societies. While Western approaches often focus on personal psychology, many traditional cultures view dreams as collective experiences that strengthen community bonds and preserve cultural wisdom.

Despite vast geographical and historical differences, certain dream themes appear consistently across cultures, suggesting fundamental human experiences that transcend cultural boundaries. The belief that dreams serve as messages from a spiritual realm emerges as one of the most widespread commonalities, though interpretations vary significantly.

Many societies view dreams as direct communication channels with divine or spiritual forces. Native American tribes like the Iroquois consider dreams as wishes from the soul that must be fulfilled to maintain spiritual harmony. Similarly, Islamic tradition holds that true dreams (ru'yā) come from Allah, while ancient Egyptians believed dreams carried messages from their deities through symbolic imagery.

However, the way these spiritual messages manifest differs notably between cultures. Hindu tradition recognizes dreams as one of four states of consciousness, alongside waking, deep sleep, and transcendental awareness. Japanese Shinto practitioners historically used dream divination (reiden) to receive guidance from kami spirits, often through specific ritual preparations.

The integration of dreams into daily life also varies significantly across cultures. Some societies, like certain Amazonian tribes, consider dream experiences as real as waking events, incorporating them into decision-making processes about hunting, warfare, and social interactions. In contrast, contemporary Western cultures often regard dreams as primarily psychological phenomena, separate from daily reality.

Traditional Chinese culture demonstrates a middle ground, where dreams might carry spiritual significance but are also interpreted through the lens of physical well-being, connected to the balance of qi (life force) in the body. This holistic approach combines spiritual meaning with practical health implications.

The intensity of dream significance also varies. While some cultures mandate immediate action based on dream content, others view dreams as subtle suggestions requiring careful interpretation. The Australian Aborigines' connection to the Dreamtime represents perhaps the most integrated relationship, where dreams fundamentally shape understanding of both past and present reality.

These diverse approaches to dream interpretation reflect each society's broader worldview and values, while maintaining the common thread of dreams as meaningful experiences worthy of attention and analysis. Understanding these cultural variations provides valuable context for modern dream exploration, offering multiple frameworks through which to examine our own dream experiences.

Religious traditions have profoundly shaped how different cultures interpret and value dreams, creating intricate frameworks for understanding these nocturnal experiences. In Islamic tradition, dreams hold particular significance, with authentic dreams (ru'yā) considered one of the forty-six parts of prophecy. Muslims often seek meaning in their dreams through established interpretative guidelines dating back to the Prophet Muhammad's teachings.

The Islamic perspective categorizes dreams into three types: divine messages, reflections of personal desires, and satanic deceptions. True divine dreams arrive with crystal clarity, leaving a lasting impression unlike regular dreams. Many Muslims consult religious scholars or dream interpretation books rooted in prophetic traditions, especially when dreams contain religious symbols or Quranic verses.

Hindu philosophy presents a distinct approach, viewing dreams as karmic reflections of past actions and future possibilities. The ancient texts of Upanishads describe dreams as an intermediate state of consciousness, bridging the physical and spiritual realms. According to Hindu belief, the soul temporarily detaches from the body during sleep, allowing it to experience different planes of existence and receive messages from the divine.

The concept of karma influences Hindu dream interpretation significantly. Dreams often serve as indicators of one's karmic balance, with certain dream symbols considered auspicious or inauspicious based on traditional Sanskrit texts. For instance, dreaming of deities, cows, or holy men traditionally signals positive karma, while dreams of loss or darkness might suggest karmic obstacles requiring attention.

In both traditions, dreams function as spiritual barometers, offering insights into one's relationship with the divine and moral standing. However, their interpretative approaches differ notably. Islamic dream interpretation follows more structured guidelines, while Hindu interpretation allows for greater flexibility based on individual spiritual development and karmic context.

These religious perspectives demonstrate how cultural beliefs shape dream interpretation, offering their followers specific frameworks for understanding and acting upon dream experiences. While modern psychological approaches might view dreams differently, these religious interpretations remain deeply meaningful to millions of practitioners worldwide, influencing how they engage with and understand their dream experiences.

Historical events and societal structures have profoundly shaped how different cultures understand and value dreams. Ancient Greek and Roman societies exemplify how dreams became woven into the fabric of civic and religious life. In these classical civilizations, dreams served multiple functions - from divine messages to medical diagnoses.

The Greeks established dedicated sleep temples called Asclepions, where people would sleep in hopes of receiving healing dreams from Asclepius, the god of medicine. These temples weren't merely spiritual centers but functioned as early healthcare facilities. Priests would interpret visitors' dreams to prescribe treatments, creating one of the first systematic approaches to using dreams for medical purposes.

Roman culture adopted many Greek practices but developed their own distinctive relationship with dreams. Roman military commanders often consulted dream interpreters before battles, and political decisions could be influenced by significant dreams. The Romans documented these experiences meticulously, leaving historical records that reveal how dreams shaped their society's major decisions.

The impact of colonialism on indigenous dream practices presents a darker chapter in dream interpretation history. Many indigenous cultures traditionally viewed dreams as essential connections to ancestral wisdom and spiritual guidance. Colonial powers often dismissed or actively suppressed these practices, labeling them as primitive or superstitious.

For instance, Native American tribes historically used dreams for community decision-making and healing practices. Colonial authorities banned many of these dream-centered ceremonies, forcing them underground or leading to their loss. Similar patterns emerged in Australian Aboriginal communities, where dreamtime traditions faced systematic suppression under colonial rule.

This colonial impact continues to influence modern dream interpretation. Many indigenous communities now struggle to recover their traditional dream practices, while others maintain them secretly alongside more "acceptable" Western approaches. The loss of these ancient dream interpretation methods represents not just a spiritual loss but the erosion of unique ways of understanding human consciousness and community healing.

Today's dream interpretation landscape reflects this complex historical interplay. While some traditional practices have been lost or altered, others persist, often adapting to incorporate both ancestral wisdom and contemporary understanding. This evolution demonstrates how dream interpretation continues to reflect and respond to changing social and historical contexts.

17

The Role
of Dreams
in Indigenous
Traditions

Indigenous cultures across the world have developed sophisticated practices around dreams, viewing them as gateways to spiritual wisdom and communal healing. These traditions offer profound insights into how dreams can serve both individual and collective purposes.

Native American vision quests exemplify the deep connection between dreams and spiritual growth. Young tribe members traditionally embark on multi-day fasts in isolated natural settings, seeking dream visions to reveal their life purpose. They prepare through purification rituals, often including sweat lodge ceremonies and sacred tobacco offerings. During these quests, dreams take on heightened significance, believed to carry messages from spirit guides and ancestors.

The Lakota people practice hanbleceya, or "crying for a vision," where seekers spend four days and nights alone on a hill, fasting and praying. Their dreams during this period are considered sacred communications, offering guidance about their role within the tribe and connection to the natural world.

Among the Maori of New Zealand, dream practices weave into their concept of matakite - spiritual sight or clairvoyance. Tohunga, their spiritual experts, interpret dreams as messages from tupuna (ancestors) and use these insights for community healing. Traditional Maori dream rituals often involve sleeping near sacred sites or marae (meeting grounds), where the boundary between the physical and spiritual worlds is believed to be thinner.

Maori healers particularly value moemoea (significant dreams), incorporating them into healing practices. They may prescribe specific sleeping locations or times based on dream messages, using natural elements like greenstone or flowing water to enhance dream connections. These practices emphasize the collective nature of dream wisdom - individual dreams often contain messages relevant to family and tribal wellbeing.

These indigenous approaches share common threads: they view dreams as natural bridges between physical and spiritual realms, emphasize preparation and intention-setting before seeking dream guidance, and recognize dreams as tools for both personal and community healing. Unlike modern Western approaches that often focus solely on individual psychology, these traditions understand dreams within a broader context of spiritual and communal relationships.

In many indigenous societies, dreams aren't relegated to nighttime curiosities but serve as vital tools for daily survival and decision-making. The Inuit people of the Arctic regions demonstrate this practical integration of dream wisdom particularly well.

Inuit hunters pay careful attention to their dreams before embarking on hunting expeditions. They believe dreams provide essential information about weather patterns, animal movements, and potential dangers. A dream of shifting ice might warn of unstable conditions, while visions of specific animals often indicate their likely locations. These dream-based insights complement their extensive knowledge of wildlife patterns and environmental signs.

During the dark Arctic winters, when navigation becomes especially challenging, the Inuit have historically relied on dreams to help guide their travel routes. Dreams of certain landmarks or natural features often influence their choice of paths across the tundra. They view these dreams not as supernatural phenomena but as natural extensions of their observational skills, where the subconscious mind processes subtle environmental cues noticed during waking hours.

The practice extends beyond individual hunters to benefit entire communities. When an Inuit hunter dreams of abundant seals in a particular location, this information is shared with the community, influencing collective hunting strategies. These dreams aren't treated as mere suggestions but as practical intelligence to be weighed alongside other environmental indicators.

Weather prediction through dreams plays a crucial role in daily planning. The Inuit have observed correlations between specific dream symbols and upcoming weather patterns. For instance, dreams of certain cloud formations or wind directions are taken as reliable indicators of imminent weather changes, helping communities prepare for storms or favorable hunting conditions.

This integration of dreams into daily life reflects a holistic approach to survival, where dream wisdom complements rather than replaces practical knowledge. Modern Inuit communities continue to value these traditional dream practices, especially in regions where weather technology may be unreliable or inaccessible. Their experience demonstrates how dreams can serve as practical tools for environmental awareness and community survival.

Dreams weave through the tapestry of Aboriginal Australian culture as essential threads in their storytelling traditions, particularly within the complex system of songlines. These ancient oral maps contain vital information about landscapes, resources, and spiritual knowledge, often transmitted through dream experiences.

In Aboriginal culture, the Dreamtime represents more than just nocturnal visions - it encompasses the fundamental creation period when ancestral beings shaped the land and established laws. Dreams serve as bridges to this spiritual dimension, allowing individuals to access and maintain these crucial cultural narratives.

Songlines, also known as dreaming tracks, form intricate pathways across the Australian continent. These oral traditions combine geographic knowledge with spiritual wisdom, often revealed through dreams. A songline might describe the location of water sources through dream symbols of rainbow serpents, or mark dangerous territories through dreams of specific animal spirits.

The preservation of these dream-infused stories follows strict protocols. Elders receive songs and stories through dreams, maintaining their accuracy through careful repetition and transmission to younger generations. These dreams often contain precise details about navigation, survival skills, and sacred sites, ensuring practical knowledge remains intact alongside spiritual teachings.

Dreams play a crucial role in validating and refreshing these oral traditions. When multiple community members experience similar dreams about specific locations or events mentioned in songlines, it reinforces the accuracy and importance of these cultural narratives. This collective dream experience helps maintain the integrity of stories across generations.

Modern Aboriginal communities continue to rely on dream-informed storytelling to preserve their cultural heritage. Dreams provide ongoing connections to ancestral wisdom, helping communities adapt traditional knowledge to contemporary challenges while maintaining their cultural identity.

The relationship between dreams and storytelling in Aboriginal culture demonstrates how dreams can serve as powerful tools for cultural preservation, combining practical survival knowledge with spiritual wisdom in ways that remain relevant and vital to this day.

Indigenous cultures worldwide share a profound understanding of dreams as gateways to spiritual realms, viewing them not merely as nightly experiences but as sacred channels of communication. Dreams serve as bridges between the physical and spiritual worlds, offering direct connections to ancestral wisdom and divine guidance.

Many indigenous peoples believe ancestors actively communicate through dreams, sharing warnings, blessings, and cultural knowledge. The Lakota people, for instance, recognize dreams where deceased relatives appear as significant spiritual messages requiring careful attention and interpretation. These visitations often occur during times of personal or community crisis, providing guidance when most needed.

Dreams hold particular significance in shamanic practices, where they function as tools for spiritual healing and community guidance. Shamans undergo extensive training to develop their ability to intentionally journey through dream states, accessing deeper spiritual insights. Through these controlled dream experiences, they gather information about healing practices, community decisions, and maintaining harmony with the natural world.

The practice of dream incubation - deliberately seeking spiritual guidance through dreams - appears consistently across indigenous traditions. Sacred spaces, often caves or specially constructed structures, serve as locations where individuals retreat to receive divine messages through dreams. These practices typically involve specific preparations, including fasting, meditation, or ritual cleansing to enhance spiritual receptivity.

Indigenous peoples recognize different categories of spiritual dreams, each serving distinct purposes. Prophetic dreams warn of future events or changes in weather patterns affecting hunting and gathering. Healing dreams reveal traditional medicine practices or specific treatments for ailments. Initiation dreams mark important life transitions, particularly for those called to spiritual leadership roles.

The interpretation of spiritual dreams in indigenous cultures follows established protocols, often requiring consultation with community elders or spiritual leaders. These interpretations consider not only the dream's content but also its timing, the dreamer's life circumstances, and its potential significance for the broader community. Natural symbols within dreams - animals, weather patterns, or landscape features - carry specific spiritual meanings rooted in cultural traditions and ancestral teachings.

18

Modern Interpretations in Eastern Philosophies

E astern spiritual traditions offer profound insights into dreams as pathways to enlightenment, viewing them not merely as nightly phenomena but as opportunities for deeper spiritual understanding. In Zen Buddhism, dreams often serve as living koans - paradoxical riddles that transcend logical thinking and lead to sudden enlightenment.

Zen practitioners approach dreams with the same mindful attention they bring to meditation. Rather than analyzing dreams for symbolic meaning, they observe them as direct expressions of mind, treating each dream as a potential doorway to awakening. The seeming contradictions within dreams mirror the paradoxical nature of koans, challenging practitioners to move beyond dualistic thinking.

In Taoist tradition, dreams represent opportunities to cultivate and refine inner energy, or qi. Taoists developed specific practices for maintaining awareness during sleep, believing that consciousness continues to evolve through dream states. These practices include specialized breathing techniques performed before sleep and methods for remaining mindfully present while transitioning between waking and dreaming states.

Taoists view dreams as reflections of the natural balance between yin and yang energies within the practitioner. Disturbing dreams might indicate an imbalance requiring attention, while peaceful dreams suggest harmony with the Tao. Through careful observation of dream patterns, practitioners gain insights into their spiritual development and areas needing refinement.

Both traditions emphasize the importance of approaching dreams without attachment or judgment. Rather than seeking specific interpretations or outcomes, practitioners cultivate a state of open awareness that allows dreams to reveal their teachings naturally. This non-striving attitude aligns with core Eastern philosophical principles of wu-wei (non-doing) and mindful presence.

The integration of dreams into daily spiritual practice takes various forms in Eastern traditions. Some monasteries maintain dream journals not to analyze content, but to track the practitioner's evolving relationship with consciousness itself. Others incorporate dream experiences into morning meditation sessions, treating them as equal to waking experiences in their potential for insight.

While Western psychology has deeply influenced modern approaches to dream interpretation, Eastern philosophies have long integrated psychological insights in their own unique ways. The meeting of these traditions has created rich frameworks for understanding the mind through dreams.

Carl Jung's work particularly resonates with Eastern perspectives, as his concept of the collective unconscious parallels Buddhist teachings about interconnected consciousness. Jung's travels to India and his study of Eastern philosophy influenced his theories about archetypes and symbolism, creating bridges between Western psychological analysis and Eastern spiritual wisdom.

Modern Eastern dream analysis often combines traditional meditation practices with psychological self-reflection. For instance, practitioners might use mindfulness techniques to observe their emotional responses to dreams while considering the psychological symbolism present. This integrated approach helps identify patterns in both conscious and unconscious mental processes.

Eastern traditions emphasize the inseparability of mind and body, viewing dreams as expressions of this unity. Unlike Western psychology's tendency to compartmentalize different aspects of human experience, Eastern approaches treat dreams as holistic manifestations of one's total being. This perspective aligns with contemporary psychological research on the mind-body connection.

The Buddhist concept of "empty mind" provides a unique lens for psychological dream interpretation. Rather than attempting to fill dreams with meaning, practitioners are encouraged to observe their dreams with detached awareness, noting how the mind creates and clings to various interpretations. This approach helps identify psychological patterns and attachments that might otherwise go unnoticed.

Eastern philosophy also influences how modern practitioners view the therapeutic potential of dreams. Instead of seeing dreams primarily as problems to be solved or symptoms to be treated, Eastern-influenced approaches treat dreams as natural expressions of psychological processes that can lead to greater self-understanding when observed with proper attention and awareness.

This integration of Eastern wisdom with psychological insights offers practitioners a more complete toolkit for understanding their dreams, combining the analytical precision of Western psychology with the contemplative depth of Eastern traditions.

Contemporary Eastern thinkers have significantly shaped modern approaches to dream interpretation, particularly through their emphasis on mindfulness and present-moment awareness. Thich Nhat Hanh's teachings stand out for their practical application to dream work, offering accessible methods for understanding our nocturnal experiences.

Thich Nhat Hanh's concept of "interbeing" - the interconnectedness of all phenomena - provides a fresh perspective on dream interpretation. Rather than viewing dreams as isolated events, his approach encourages seeing them as part of our wider consciousness, connected to our daily experiences, relationships, and environment. This perspective helps practitioners recognize how their dreams reflect not just personal concerns, but also their connections to family, community, and the natural world.

His teachings on mindful breathing and walking meditation have been adapted for dream work. By applying these techniques before sleep, practitioners report improved dream recall and greater awareness during dreams. The simple act of following one's breath while focusing on the present moment creates a mental clarity that often carries into dream states.

Thich Nhat Hanh's emphasis on gentle awareness, rather than forceful analysis, has influenced how many approach dream interpretation. Instead of aggressively seeking meaning, his methods encourage sitting with dream images and allowing understanding to arise naturally. This approach reduces anxiety about dream interpretation and creates space for deeper insights to emerge.

His concept of "mindful consumption" extends to how we process dream content. Just as we're encouraged to be mindful of what we eat and watch, his teachings suggest being mindful of how we interpret and integrate dream experiences. This includes being aware of cultural biases and personal assumptions that might color our understanding of dream symbols.

When applying Thich Nhat Hanh's teachings to practical dream work, mindful breathing becomes a powerful tool for sleep preparation. By focusing on each breath, we calm our racing thoughts and create optimal conditions for dream recall. During the process of recording dreams, practicing non-judgmental awareness helps capture details without immediate interpretation or criticism.

Approaching dream symbols with gentle curiosity allows their meanings to unfold naturally. Rather than forcing interpretations based on dream dictionaries or preset meanings, this method honors the personal significance of each symbol. Understanding dreams through the lens of interbeing reveals how dream content connects to various aspects of our lives - from daily experiences to deeper emotional states.

Present-moment awareness during dream recall enhances our ability to remember and work with dream content. Instead of straining to remember details, maintaining mindful awareness helps preserve the delicate threads of dream memories as they surface into consciousness.

The globalization of dream interpretation has created a fascinating fusion between Eastern spiritual traditions and Western psychological approaches. Traditional Eastern views, which often emphasized collective wisdom and spiritual guidance through dreams, have evolved to incorporate modern psychological frameworks while maintaining their cultural essence.

In contemporary Japan, for instance, traditional Shinto beliefs about dreams as divine messages now coexist with psychoanalytic approaches. Professional dream workers often blend ancient techniques like sutra chanting with cognitive behavioral therapy methods. This integration reflects a broader trend across Asia, where ancient wisdom meets modern science in dream interpretation practices.

The influence of Western psychology has particularly shaped how Eastern practitioners approach dream work in clinical settings. Many Asian universities now offer courses that combine traditional dream interpretation methods with Jungian psychology and neuroscientific research. This academic fusion has led to innovative research methodologies that honor both perspectives.

Western psychological theories have found particular resonance in urban Asian settings, where stress management and mental health awareness are growing priorities. Dream interpretation workshops in cities like Seoul and Singapore often incorporate elements of both Eastern mindfulness practices and Western psychological frameworks, creating a comprehensive approach that appeals to modern sensibilities while respecting traditional values.

However, this integration hasn't been without challenges. Some traditional practitioners express concern about the dilution of ancient wisdom, while others celebrate the enhanced understanding that comes from combining multiple perspectives. The key has been finding balance - maintaining the essence of Eastern spiritual approaches while benefiting from Western psychological insights.

Modern Eastern dream studies increasingly acknowledge the value of both perspectives: the Western focus on individual psychology and the Eastern emphasis on collective consciousness and spiritual growth. This synthesis has created more nuanced approaches to dream interpretation that consider both personal psychological dynamics and broader spiritual dimensions.

The result is a more holistic approach to dream interpretation that resonates with contemporary audiences while preserving the depth of traditional Eastern wisdom. This evolution reflects a broader global trend toward integrating different cultural perspectives in psychological and spiritual practices.

19

Western Approaches to Dream Analysis

The Western understanding of dreams has undergone a remarkable transformation over centuries, shifting from supernatural beliefs to scientific inquiry. In ancient Greece and Rome, dreams held divine significance - viewed as messages from the gods or glimpses into the future. Temples dedicated to Asclepius, the god of healing, hosted ritual dream incubation where seekers slept in sacred spaces awaiting divine guidance through their dreams.

Medieval European society largely viewed dreams through a Christian lens, categorizing them as either divine prophecy or demonic temptation. Dream interpretation manuals from this period focused on religious symbolism and moral instruction. The Renaissance period began challenging these purely spiritual interpretations, as scholars started examining dreams through a more rational lens.

The 19th century marked a pivotal shift in dream interpretation. The rise of scientific thinking and psychological inquiry transformed dreams from mystical experiences into windows to the unconscious mind. This era saw the emergence of dream research as a legitimate field of study, with scientists documenting dream patterns and seeking physiological explanations for dream experiences.

Sigmund Freud's publication of "The Interpretation of Dreams" in 1900 revolutionized Western understanding of dreams. His psychoanalytic approach proposed that dreams represented unconscious wishes and repressed desires. Freud introduced concepts like dream symbolism, manifest content (the literal dream narrative) versus latent content (hidden meanings), and dream censorship - where the mind disguises uncomfortable thoughts through symbolic representation.

Freud's theory of wish fulfillment suggested that dreams serve as a safety valve for repressed desires. He argued that even unpleasant dreams ultimately represented wish fulfillment, though often in disguised forms. This revolutionary perspective shifted dream interpretation from external divine messages to internal psychological processes, establishing dreams as valuable tools for understanding the human psyche.

The medical and scientific communities initially met Freud's theories with skepticism, but his work laid the groundwork for modern psychological approaches to dream interpretation. His emphasis on systematic analysis and symbolic understanding continues to influence contemporary dream work, though many of his specific interpretations have been challenged or modified by subsequent research.

Contemporary Western approaches to dream analysis blend traditional psychological insights with evidence-based practices. Professional therapists and self-help practitioners increasingly recognize dream journaling as a powerful tool for personal growth and emotional healing. This systematic recording of dreams provides valuable data for both individual reflection and therapeutic discussion.

Modern dream journaling extends beyond simple narrative recording. Practitioners often include emotional states, physical sensations, and life events surrounding the dream. This comprehensive approach helps identify patterns between waking experiences and dream content. For example, recording stress levels before sleep might reveal correlations with specific dream themes or intensity.

In therapeutic settings, dream journals serve multiple purposes. Therapists use these records to track progress in addressing anxiety, depression, or trauma. The journal becomes a shared reference point, allowing both client and therapist to explore recurring symbols or themes. This collaborative analysis often reveals insights that might be missed in traditional talk therapy alone.

Digital technology has revolutionized dream journaling practices. Smartphone apps now offer structured templates for recording dreams, complete with emotion tracking, symbol tagging, and pattern recognition features. These tools help users identify connections between their dreams and daily life, making the practice more accessible to those seeking self-directed growth.

Professional dream groups and workshops frequently incorporate journaling as a core practice. Participants learn specific techniques for detailed dream documentation, such as recording dreams in present tense to maintain emotional immediacy, or using color-coding systems to track different dream elements. These structured approaches help practitioners develop deeper awareness of their dream patterns and their potential significance.

Research indicates that consistent dream journaling can improve dream recall and emotional awareness. Regular practitioners often report increased ability to recognize personal dream symbols and their meanings, leading to better understanding of their subconscious patterns and concerns. This enhanced self-awareness aligns with the goals of many therapeutic approaches, making dream journaling a valuable complement to traditional mental health practices.

Dreams have profoundly shaped Western artistic expression while simultaneously captivating scientific inquiry. Artists and scientists approach dreams from different angles, yet both perspectives offer valuable insights into the nature of human consciousness and creativity.

In Western literature, dreams have served as powerful narrative devices and sources of inspiration. Mary Shelley conceived the idea for "Frankenstein" during a vivid dream, while Robert Louis Stevenson's "Dr. Jekyll and Mr. Hyde" emerged from a nightmare. These works reflect how dreams can crystallize complex psychological themes into compelling narratives. Similarly, Salvador Dali's surrealist paintings capture dream-like distortions of reality, demonstrating how dreams can break conventional artistic boundaries and spark new forms of expression.

Modern neuroscience has begun unraveling the biological basis of dream creativity. Brain imaging studies reveal increased activity in regions associated with visual processing and emotional regulation during REM sleep. This heightened neural activity often correlates with novel problem-solving abilities and creative insights. Research shows that the brain's pattern-recognition systems operate differently during dreams, allowing for unique connections between seemingly unrelated concepts.

The intersection of art and science in dream studies has led to innovative therapeutic approaches. Art therapy now incorporates dream imagery as a tool for emotional processing, while sleep laboratories study how artistic expression influences dream content. This collaboration between creative and analytical approaches provides a more comprehensive understanding of how dreams function in human consciousness.

Recent neuropsychological studies have identified specific brain wave patterns associated with creative problem-solving during dreams. These findings suggest that the dream state may serve as an optimal environment for creative breakthroughs, as the brain becomes free from conventional logical constraints. Scientists have documented cases where complex mathematical problems and scientific innovations emerged through dream insights, supporting the notion that dreams can enhance cognitive flexibility and creative thinking.

These discoveries validate what artists have long intuited - that dreams offer a unique mental space where creativity flourishes. By understanding both the scientific mechanisms and artistic manifestations of dreams, we gain a deeper appreciation for their role in human cognition and cultural expression.

Dreams permeate Western popular culture, shaping storytelling across various media forms. Hollywood has particularly embraced dreams as a versatile narrative device, using them to explore complex themes and push visual boundaries. Films like "Inception" demonstrate how dreams-within-dreams can create layered storytelling structures, while "A Nightmare on Elm Street" exploits the vulnerability we feel during sleep. These portrayals often emphasize the surreal aspects of dreams, using advanced special effects to create impossible landscapes and physics-defying sequences that capture the fluid nature of dream logic.

Western literature has long used dreams as a gateway to explore deeper psychological and philosophical concepts. Lewis Carroll's "Alice in Wonderland" presents a dream world that challenges social conventions and reality itself, using dream logic to critique Victorian society. Modern novels continue this tradition, with authors like Neil Gaiman incorporating dream elements to blur the lines between reality and fantasy in works like "The Sandman" series.

Television shows frequently employ dream sequences to reveal characters' hidden fears and desires without directly affecting the main plot. These sequences often use distinct visual styles, such as soft focus or altered color palettes, to signal the transition into dream states. Popular shows like "The Sopranos" have used dreams extensively to explore characters' subconscious minds and provide psychological insight.

The influence of dream imagery extends into advertising and music videos, where surreal elements create memorable visual experiences that capture attention. Advertisers often use dream-like scenarios to associate their products with aspirational lifestyles or emotional states, playing on the universal experience of dreaming to create relatable content.

Video games have embraced dreams as both setting and mechanic, creating interactive experiences that allow players to explore dream worlds firsthand. Games like "LittleBigPlanet" and "Dreams" enable users to create their own dream-like environments, fostering creative expression through digital dreamscapes.

These cultural representations reflect society's ongoing fascination with dreams while simultaneously shaping public understanding of dream experiences. Though often dramatized for entertainment value, these portrayals help normalize discussion of dreams and their potential significance in daily life.

20

Healing Emotional Trauma Through Dream Work

Dreams serve as a natural mechanism for processing traumatic experiences, often bringing difficult memories to the surface when the conscious mind feels safe enough to confront them. The brain uses REM sleep to sort through emotional experiences, allowing trauma to emerge in symbolic forms that feel less threatening than direct memories.

Recurring dreams frequently point to unresolved trauma. A person who survived a car accident might repeatedly dream of being unable to stop a moving vehicle, while someone who experienced emotional abandonment could have recurring dreams of being lost in empty buildings. These patterns aren't random - they represent the psyche's attempt to process and integrate difficult experiences.

The brain creates these scenarios during REM sleep when the amygdala, responsible for processing emotions, becomes highly active while the prefrontal cortex, which normally inhibits strong emotional responses, reduces its activity. This unique state allows traumatic memories to surface without triggering the same level of distress experienced during waking hours.

Dreams can present trauma in metaphorical ways that make processing easier. Instead of reliving the exact traumatic event, the brain might transform it into symbolic scenarios. Water often represents overwhelming emotions, while dark spaces might symbolize fear or uncertainty. These symbols allow the mind to approach difficult memories indirectly, making them more manageable to process.

The therapeutic potential of revisiting traumatic dreams lies in their ability to provide a safe space for confronting painful memories. During REM sleep, the body naturally produces stress-relieving chemicals while keeping muscles paralyzed, creating ideal conditions for processing trauma without physical stress responses. This biological safety net allows the mind to explore difficult memories while maintaining a degree of emotional distance.

Working with traumatic dreams in therapy can lead to breakthrough insights. Writing down recurring dream patterns helps identify triggers and emotional patterns that need attention. Over time, as trauma processing progresses, these dreams often transform - becoming less intense or taking on new, more empowering forms.

Dream re-scripting offers a powerful tool for transforming disturbing dreams into opportunities for emotional healing. The process works by consciously reimagining troubling dream scenarios while awake, creating new pathways in the brain that can influence future dream patterns.

To begin re-scripting a dream, first identify the most distressing elements. A common example involves being chased - instead of remaining powerless, visualize turning to face the pursuer or discovering you can fly away. Another example might transform a dream of falling into one of floating or gracefully landing. The key lies in maintaining the core elements while changing your response to them.

The re-scripting process follows specific steps. Start by writing down the original dream in detail, noting particularly triggering moments. Then, pause at these points and consciously imagine alternative outcomes. Someone who frequently dreams of being trapped might envision walls becoming transparent or discovering they can walk through them. The new ending should feel empowering but realistic within the dream's context.

Visualization exercises strengthen this practice. Before sleep, spend 5-10 minutes mentally rehearsing your preferred dream ending. Picture specific details - colors, sounds, physical sensations. If you dream of being unable to speak during a presentation, imagine your voice becoming clear and strong, the audience responding positively. For dreams about losing control of a vehicle, envision smoothly steering to safety.

The brain responds to these mental rehearsals similarly to actual experiences. Regular practice creates new neural pathways, making it more likely for future dreams to incorporate these empowering elements. Like learning any new skill, consistency matters more than duration - even brief daily visualization sessions can yield significant results.

When crafting new dream endings, focus on realistic empowerment rather than magical solutions. Instead of suddenly becoming invincible, imagine finding inner strength or calling for help. This approach helps the brain accept and integrate the new scenarios more readily, leading to lasting changes in dream patterns.

Dream work plays a vital role in modern therapeutic practices, particularly when addressing trauma. Therapists often incorporate dream analysis to help clients process difficult experiences that may be too overwhelming to confront directly while awake. The subconscious mind frequently presents these challenges through symbolic imagery, allowing for gentler exploration of traumatic memories.

In clinical settings, therapists typically begin by establishing a safe environment where clients feel comfortable sharing their dreams. Rather than immediately interpreting dream content, the focus remains on allowing clients to explore their own associations and emotions connected to dream imagery. This approach proves especially effective with trauma survivors who may struggle to verbalize their experiences.

Recent studies have documented successful cases where dream work facilitated breakthrough moments in trauma therapy. For instance, recurring dreams of natural disasters often symbolize overwhelming past experiences. Through guided exploration of these dreams, clients can gradually process their trauma responses in a contained, therapeutic setting. Another common pattern involves dreams of being pursued, which frequently represent unresolved fight-or-flight responses to past threats.

Several effective therapeutic approaches help individuals work with challenging dream content. The process of drawing or painting dream scenes provides a tangible way to externalize difficult emotions that may feel overwhelming when approached directly. Writing detailed dream narratives from multiple perspectives allows for a deeper understanding of the dream's emotional landscape. Creating timeline connections between dreams and significant life events helps identify patterns and triggers that may influence dream content.

The practice of tracking recurring symbols proves particularly valuable, as these symbols often evolve throughout the therapeutic journey, reflecting internal changes and healing. Mindfulness techniques serve as essential tools when exploring challenging dream material, helping maintain present-moment awareness while processing difficult content. These practices create a foundation of emotional stability that supports deeper dream exploration.

Through consistent dream work, individuals often notice shifts in their dream patterns that parallel their healing journey. Natural disaster dreams may become less intense or transform into scenes of rebuilding and renewal. Chase dreams might evolve to include moments of empowerment or successful confrontation, reflecting growing emotional resilience.

The therapeutic setting provides crucial support for this work, offering professional guidance when dreams trigger intense emotional responses. Therapists help clients develop coping strategies for managing anxiety that may arise during dream exploration. They also assist in recognizing patterns between dream content and daily life stressors, enabling clients to better understand their trauma responses.

For maximum therapeutic benefit, dream work often combines with other evidence-based trauma treatments. This integrated approach allows clients to process trauma through multiple channels, with dreams offering unique insights into their healing journey. The goal remains focused on empowering clients to understand and transform their relationship with traumatic memories, using dreams as a valuable tool in their recovery process.

Dream healing offers powerful tools for personal growth and emotional recovery that you can practice at home. While professional guidance remains valuable for processing severe trauma, gentle self-guided techniques can support your healing journey.

Dream meditation serves as an effective starting point. Before sleep, create a quiet space and sit comfortably with eyes closed. Focus on your breath while setting an intention to explore unresolved emotions through your dreams. This practice helps prepare your mind for therapeutic dreaming.

When you first wake up, the key is remaining motionless to maintain that delicate bridge between sleep and wakefulness. This allows you to notice physical sensations and emotional residue from your dreams without immediately dismissing or analyzing them. Deep, mindful breathing helps process any intense feelings that surface during this transition. If dream content feels particularly overwhelming, grounding techniques like focusing on your immediate environment - the weight of your blanket, morning birds chirping, sunlight filtering through curtains - can help restore emotional balance.

A structured journaling practice creates a safe container for exploring dream content. Begin entries with concrete details - vivid colors, recurring symbols, and emotional tones that stood out. From this foundation, deeper exploration becomes possible through targeted reflection questions. Consider which emotions emerged most strongly and where you physically felt them in your body. Examine how these feelings connect to past experiences or current life situations. Imagine what you might say to dream characters if given the chance for dialogue. Finally, consider how this dream could be supporting your healing journey.

This approach to dream work acknowledges both the universal patterns in how humans process dreams and the deeply personal nature of each individual's dream experiences. By staying present with dream content while maintaining healthy boundaries, you can engage with dreams as tools for growth and healing in a way that feels safe and meaningful.

Create distance from difficult content by writing in third person or from different perspectives. This technique allows processing trauma indirectly. For example, describe a challenging dream as if telling someone else's story.

Track patterns in your dream journal over time. Notice recurring symbols, emotions, or scenarios. These often point to areas needing attention in your healing journey. Look for shifts in how these patterns evolve - growing feelings of empowerment or reduced anxiety can signal progress.

Remember to practice self-care during dream exploration. Set boundaries around when and how deeply you engage with dream content. Take breaks when needed. Consider sharing your journey with trusted friends or joining dream sharing circles for support.

Through consistent practice, dreams can become allies in your healing process, offering insights and opportunities for gentle emotional release at your own pace.

21

Unlocking Personal Growth via Dreams

D reams serve as powerful mirrors reflecting the depths of our inner landscape, offering glimpses into aspects of ourselves we might overlook in waking life. Through careful observation of dream patterns, hidden strengths emerge like buried treasures waiting to be discovered.

Consider the common dream of flying - beyond its surface excitement lies potential insight into personal capabilities. A dreamer who soars effortlessly might possess untapped leadership qualities or the ability to rise above challenges. Conversely, struggling to maintain altitude in dreams could point to self-imposed limitations needing examination.

Dreams often spotlight talents through unexpected scenarios. An accountant dreams of conducting an orchestra, revealing a dormant creative spark. A shy office worker leads a successful revolution in their dreamscape, highlighting hidden charisma and leadership potential. These scenarios aren't random - they represent genuine capabilities waiting to be acknowledged and developed.

The subconscious mind excels at exposing areas for growth through dream symbolism. Recurring dreams of being unprepared for an exam might indicate perfectionist tendencies holding someone back. Dreams of being lost in familiar places could signal a need to reassess life direction or career path.

Dream symbols also illuminate unexplored desires. A corporate executive repeatedly dreams of tending a garden, revealing a yearning for more grounded, nurturing work. An artist dreams of teaching, uncovering a desire to share knowledge and mentor others. These themes emerge not as literal career mandates but as clues to unfulfilled aspects of self.

Through consistent dream observation, patterns of personal strength become apparent. Someone who regularly dreams of helping others might discover their natural counseling abilities. Dreams of solving complex puzzles could indicate untapped analytical skills. Even nightmares serve this purpose - successfully facing dream fears often translates to greater confidence in waking life.

The key lies in approaching dreams as personal growth tools rather than mysterious phenomena requiring expert interpretation. By maintaining a dream journal and noting recurring themes, anyone can begin mapping their psychological landscape and identifying areas ripe for development.

Dreams possess an extraordinary ability to illuminate paths for transformation, often revealing insights that remain hidden during waking hours. Like a compass pointing true north, dream messages can guide individuals toward authentic life directions and meaningful changes.

Career transitions frequently emerge through dream insights. A corporate executive might repeatedly dream of teaching children, the scenes filled with joy and purpose, leading them to explore education as a new career path. An office worker's recurring dreams of working with animals could spark the courage to start a pet care business. These dream messages often persist until acknowledged, growing stronger as the subconscious mind pushes for positive change.

Dreams also highlight necessary lifestyle adjustments. Recurring dreams of missing trains or being late for important events might reveal an overcommitted schedule requiring simplification. Dreams of peaceful natural settings could signal a need to escape urban stress and seek more balance through outdoor activities.

Personal development opportunities surface through dream symbolism. Dreams of speaking confidently to large crowds might encourage someone to develop their public speaking skills. Finding oneself easily speaking foreign languages in dreams could inspire actual language study. Even challenging dreams serve this purpose - repeatedly facing and overcoming dream obstacles often translates to greater resilience in waking life.

Dreams can unveil hidden talents and interests waiting to be developed. An engineer's dreams of painting masterpieces might lead to exploring artistic hobbies. Dreams of successfully mediating conflicts could reveal natural counseling abilities. These nighttime messages often point toward fulfilling pursuits that align with authentic interests and abilities.

The transformation process begins with recognizing and acting on dream insights. Small steps, like enrolling in a single art class or volunteering at an animal shelter, allow individuals to test the waters of potential life changes. Through this gradual exploration, dreams serve as catalysts for positive growth, guiding people toward more authentic and satisfying life paths.

Dreams can become powerful tools for personal development when approached with intention and structure. By actively engaging with dream content, individuals can uncover meaningful goals and create actionable plans for growth.

Dream incubation offers a direct method for accessing guidance about personal objectives. Before sleep, focus on a specific area of desired growth - career advancement, relationship improvement, or creative development. Write this intention in a journal and visualize achieving the desired outcome. This plants the seed for dreams to provide relevant insights.

Common dream symbols often point toward growth opportunities. Climbing mountains might suggest taking on challenging projects at work. Swimming through clear water could indicate readiness to explore emotional depths. Flying dreams frequently represent breaking free from limitations. By tracking these symbols in a dream journal, patterns emerge that highlight natural directions for development.

Regular dream practice helps align conscious goals with subconscious wisdom. Set aside time each morning to record dreams and identify growth-related themes. Note recurring symbols, emotions, or scenarios that feel significant. Review these entries weekly to spot patterns that can inform goal-setting.

Transform dream insights into concrete objectives using the SMART framework:

- Specific: Define exactly what the dream suggests

- Measurable: Establish clear metrics for progress

- Achievable: Break large goals into manageable steps

- Relevant: Ensure alignment with personal values

- Time-bound: Set reasonable deadlines

For example, dreams of teaching others might translate to "Complete online certification in public speaking within 6 months." Dreams of creating art could become "Spend 30 minutes daily practicing drawing techniques."

Keep dream insights grounded in practical reality while maintaining flexibility. Dreams may suggest bold changes, but implementation often works best through gradual steps. Start with small actions that build confidence and momentum toward larger transformations.

Monitor progress through both dream content and waking achievements. As goals manifest, dreams often shift to reveal next steps or new areas for growth. This creates an ongoing dialogue between conscious ambition and subconscious guidance.

Dreams serve as natural barometers for life balance, often reflecting areas that need attention before we consciously recognize them. When work consumes too much energy, dreams might present scenes of abandoned gardens or empty homes - symbolic representations of neglected personal spaces. These images act as gentle reminders to nurture relationships and self-care routines.

Physical manifestations in dreams can point to specific imbalances. Dreams of running late or missing transportation might indicate overwhelming schedules. Recurring dreams of being unprepared for tests or presentations often suggest taking on too many responsibilities. Dreams of drowning can reflect feeling overwhelmed by emotional demands.

The subconscious mind frequently highlights neglected aspects through recurring themes. A busy executive might dream of playing with children, signaling a need for more playful activities. An artist focused solely on creative pursuits might dream of organizing files or attending meetings, suggesting a need for more structure.

Dreams can also reveal when certain life areas receive disproportionate attention. Someone overly focused on career might dream of missed family celebrations or empty personal relationships. These dreams act as course-correcting mechanisms, drawing attention to aspects of life requiring more investment.

Work-life harmony often appears in dreams through metaphorical scenarios. A dream of trying to juggle too many objects might reflect actual challenges in managing multiple life roles. Dreams of being in two places simultaneously could indicate conflicting commitments between work and personal life.

To utilize these dream insights, maintain a dream journal focusing specifically on balance-related themes. Note patterns that emerge around certain life areas - career, relationships, health, or personal growth. These patterns often reveal where attention is needed most.

The timing and frequency of certain dream themes can provide valuable information. Stress-related dreams increasing during particular periods might indicate when life balance requires adjustment. Dreams of peaceful scenarios or successful integration of different life aspects can confirm when balance is being achieved.

22

Dreams and Emotional Intelligence

D reams offer a unique window into our emotional landscape, serving as mirrors that reflect both surface feelings and deeper emotional currents we might not consciously recognize. Like a sophisticated emotional processing system, dreams filter through daily experiences, highlighting patterns in our emotional responses and reactions.

During REM sleep, the brain's emotional centers become highly active while the logical prefrontal cortex takes a step back. This creates the perfect environment for pure emotional expression, unfiltered by rational thought. A stressful work project might manifest as being chased, while unacknowledged grief could appear as searching for something lost.

Dream analysis reveals recurring emotional patterns that might otherwise go unnoticed. Someone experiencing anxiety might repeatedly dream of being unprepared for important events or arriving late to crucial appointments. These patterns often emerge before conscious awareness of the underlying emotional state takes hold.

The intensity of emotions in dreams can signal their importance in waking life. Vivid dreams filled with fear, joy, or sadness often point to significant emotional experiences requiring attention. A seemingly minor workplace conflict generating intense dream emotions might indicate deeper concerns about job security or professional identity.

Dreams serve as emotional practice grounds, allowing us to process complex feelings in a safe space. Through dream experiences, we can explore difficult emotions without real-world consequences. This emotional rehearsal helps develop greater emotional awareness and regulation skills over time.

The brain's emotional processing during dreams helps consolidate emotional memories and experiences. This consolidation contributes to emotional learning and adaptation, making dreams essential tools for developing emotional intelligence. Regular attention to dream emotions can enhance self-awareness and emotional regulation abilities.

Understanding these emotional patterns requires consistent dream recording and reflection. A dream of conflict with a colleague might reveal underlying feelings about authority or competition. Similarly, dreams of flying or success often reflect periods of emotional confidence and empowerment.

Dreams act as powerful simulators for social interactions, allowing us to experience different perspectives and emotional states that build empathy. During REM sleep, the brain processes social experiences and relationships, creating scenarios that help develop deeper understanding of others' viewpoints and feelings.

Through dreams, we often find ourselves experiencing life from another person's position. A dream might place us in the shoes of someone we've had conflict with, providing insight into their motivations and emotional state. This natural perspective-shifting builds emotional intelligence and enhances our ability to relate to others in waking life.

Dreams frequently present challenging social scenarios that require resolution. These dream experiences serve as practice grounds for developing conflict resolution skills. A dream about workplace tension might reveal alternative approaches to addressing disagreements, while dreams about family conflicts often highlight unspoken needs or feelings that need addressing.

The brain's emotional processing during dreams strengthens our capacity for empathy by allowing us to experience a wider range of emotional responses. Dreams where we feel compassion for dream characters, even those who represent people we struggle with in waking life, help expand our emotional range and understanding.

Dream scenarios often challenge our usual social responses, pushing us to develop new interpersonal skills. A dream might present a situation where we must communicate differently than our usual pattern, encouraging growth in our social abilities. These experiences can translate into improved real-world interactions, as the brain has already practiced new approaches during sleep.

The emotional rehearsal that occurs in dreams supports the development of social awareness. Dreams often highlight subtle social dynamics we might miss during waking hours, bringing attention to non-verbal cues and underlying emotional currents in our relationships. This increased awareness can lead to more nuanced and effective social interactions.

Regular attention to social themes in dreams can accelerate the development of interpersonal skills. By reflecting on dream interactions, we can identify patterns in our social responses and areas where empathy might be lacking. This awareness creates opportunities for conscious growth in our relationships and social connections.

Dreams serve as windows into our emotional landscape, offering unique opportunities to develop deeper emotional awareness and intelligence. By paying attention to the emotional content of our dreams, we can better understand our reactions, fears, and desires.

Keeping an emotion-focused dream journal helps track patterns in our emotional responses. Rather than simply recording dream events, note the feelings experienced during different dream scenarios. Was there fear when confronted by a shadow figure? Joy when flying? Anxiety when lost in a maze? These emotional markers often reflect waking life concerns and patterns.

When journaling about dreams, use an emotional scale from 1-10 to rate the intensity of different feelings. This practice helps identify which emotions appear most frequently and with what strength. Track whether certain dream symbols consistently trigger specific emotional responses. A recurring dream of being unprepared for an exam might always rate high for anxiety, revealing underlying stress about performance or preparation in waking life.

Create dedicated journal sections for different emotional themes. Group dreams by primary emotions like anger, joy, fear, or sadness. This organization helps identify recurring emotional patterns and their potential triggers. Note whether certain people, places, or situations in dreams consistently evoke particular emotional responses.

Regular reflection on dream emotions enhances self-awareness. Set aside time each morning to connect dream feelings with current life situations. If a dream provokes strong anxiety, examine what current circumstances might be triggering similar emotions. Dreams often process emotions we suppress during waking hours, bringing them to consciousness for examination.

Practice emotional mindfulness by staying with dream feelings upon waking. Instead of immediately dismissing or analyzing them, simply experience these emotions fully. This helps develop emotional tolerance and understanding. Notice physical sensations associated with dream emotions - tension, relaxation, heaviness, lightness. These bodily responses often carry important emotional information.

Through consistent practice of these techniques, dreams become valuable tools for developing emotional intelligence. They offer safe spaces to experience and process complex feelings, building greater emotional awareness and resilience.

Dreams act as natural emotional processing centers, helping build resilience through subconscious problem-solving and emotional rehearsal. When faced with challenging situations, dreams often present scenarios that allow us to practice different emotional responses in a safe environment. This mental rehearsal strengthens our ability to handle similar situations in waking life.

Research shows that individuals who pay attention to their dreams develop stronger emotional coping mechanisms. Dreams frequently offer metaphorical solutions to emotional challenges. For example, a dream about successfully navigating through a storm might provide insights into handling turbulent emotions during a difficult life transition. These symbolic experiences build confidence in managing real-world emotional challenges.

Dreams can also reveal untapped sources of inner strength. Someone struggling with self-doubt might dream of discovering a hidden room in their house, symbolizing unexplored personal resources. By recognizing and working with these dream symbols, individuals develop greater emotional flexibility and resilience.

The practice of recording and reflecting on dreams strengthens emotional awareness over time. Regular dream work helps identify emotional triggers and patterns, allowing for better emotional regulation in daily life. Those who engage with their dreams often report improved ability to recognize and manage their emotional responses before they become overwhelming.

Studies indicate that individuals who maintain dream journals show increased emotional intelligence scores over time. They demonstrate better understanding of their own emotional states and improved empathy toward others. This enhanced emotional awareness contributes to stronger relationships and better stress management.

Dreams serve as emotional warning systems, highlighting areas that need attention before they become problematic. For instance, recurring dreams of being unprepared often signal mounting anxiety that requires addressing. By heeding these dream warnings, individuals can take proactive steps to maintain emotional balance.

Through consistent dream work, people develop a broader emotional vocabulary and greater comfort with complex feelings. This expanded emotional range helps in navigating life's challenges with more confidence and adaptability. Dreams provide a natural pathway to building emotional resilience, offering insights and practice scenarios that strengthen our ability to handle life's emotional demands.

23

Astral Projection and Dream Travel

T he boundary between lucid dreaming and astral projection often blurs in discussions of consciousness exploration. While lucid dreams occur within the mind's dreamscape, astral projection involves the sensation of consciousness separating from the physical body. This perceived separation enables exploration beyond normal physical limitations.

During astral projection, experiencers report floating above their bodies or traveling to distant locations. The sensation differs from typical dream flying - instead of the fantastical freedom of dreams, astral projection maintains a more grounded perception of real-world physics and geography. An experienced projector might describe observing their sleeping body from above with precise detail of their bedroom layout, rather than the fluid, changing environments of dreams.

The astral realm presents itself as a parallel dimension overlapping physical reality. Projectors report seeing silvery cords connecting their astral and physical forms, acting as anchors during their explorations. This differs from lucid dreams where the dreamer remains fully immersed in the dream environment without maintaining a connection to their physical body.

Unlike the creative control possible in lucid dreams, astral projection often feels more like objective observation. While lucid dreamers can reshape their environment at will, astral projectors describe themselves as visitors observing but not controlling the astral plane. The experience maintains consistent rules and geography more aligned with physical reality than dream logic.

The state of consciousness during astral projection differs from both normal dreams and lucidity. Projectors report heightened awareness and clarity beyond even lucid dreams, with sharp mental faculties and memory retention. This clarity allows detailed recall of the experience, unlike the often fragmented memories of regular dreams.

Various cultures throughout history have described similar experiences of consciousness separation, though using different terminology. Ancient Egyptian texts reference the "ka" or spirit body's ability to travel while the physical body sleeps. Tibetan Buddhist practices include deliberate cultivation of consciousness projection through advanced meditation techniques.

The practice of astral projection requires patience, dedication, and specific techniques refined over centuries of exploration. The most accessible method, known as the rope technique, provides a structured approach for those seeking to experience consciousness separation.

To begin the rope technique, create optimal conditions by lying flat on your back in a quiet, dimly lit room. Relax each muscle group systematically, starting from the toes and moving upward to the crown of the head. As physical tension releases, maintain awareness while allowing the body to drift toward sleep. This delicate balance between relaxation and consciousness creates the ideal state for projection.

Imagine a thick rope hanging directly above your chest. Rather than visualizing the rope, focus on the tactile sensation of gripping it with your astral hands. The physical body remains still while you mentally reach up and pull down on the rope, hand over hand. This climbing motion helps initiate the separation between physical and astral forms.

The sensation of separation often begins with vibrations or a feeling of lightness. Some practitioners report hearing buzzing sounds or experiencing sleep paralysis during this phase. Continue the rope-climbing visualization while remaining calm and focused, allowing these sensations to develop naturally without resistance.

Visualizing the astral body requires careful attention to detail. Begin by imagining an exact energetic duplicate of your physical form, positioned slightly above your body. Focus on the sensation of this subtle form, noting its lighter density compared to the physical body. Practice transferring your awareness between the physical and astral bodies, gradually strengthening the connection to the astral form.

Movement in the astral state starts with small actions. Focus first on lifting the astral arms or legs while the physical body remains still. As confidence grows, attempt sitting up with the astral body or rolling to one side. These initial movements often trigger the complete separation experience. Maintain steady breathing and calm focus throughout the process, as excitement or fear can disrupt the delicate state of projection.

During dream travel experiences, consciousness expands beyond ordinary physical limitations, allowing for profound encounters and insights. These journeys often reveal spiritual guides who appear as archetypal figures - wise elders, luminous beings, or animal totems. Each guide emerges uniquely suited to the dreamer's current life challenges and spiritual development level.

Dream travel frequently occurs in landscapes that transcend physical reality - crystalline cities floating in cosmic void, ancient temples pulsing with living energy, or vast libraries containing universal knowledge. These settings create opportunities for expanding awareness beyond everyday limitations. A dreamer might find themselves soaring through golden clouds or diving into oceanic depths that mirror the subconscious mind.

Through these experiences, fresh perspectives emerge as dreamers witness reality from entirely new vantage points. Someone struggling with a difficult decision might view their situation from a mountaintop, gaining clarity through literal and metaphorical elevation. Another person grappling with emotional wounds could encounter healing waters in a sacred grove, the symbolic immersion representing inner cleansing and renewal.

The transformative power of dream travel stems from its ability to bypass mental barriers and cultural conditioning. When consciousness roams freely, insights arise organically rather than through intellectual effort. A dreamer might suddenly understand a complex relationship dynamic while floating above their sleeping form, or grasp a creative solution while exploring an ethereal dimension.

These journeys also facilitate connection with higher wisdom and universal consciousness. Many report accessing knowledge that feels both ancient and intimately personal - as if remembering rather than learning something new. This direct experience of expanded awareness often catalyzes profound shifts in how dreamers view themselves and their place in the cosmos.

The perspectives gained through dream travel frequently translate into practical benefits in waking life. Someone might return with renewed courage to pursue a calling, deeper compassion for others, or enhanced problem-solving abilities. These experiences can dissolve limiting beliefs and expand what dreamers believe possible for themselves and their world.

Encounters with deceased loved ones occur in settings that feel both familiar and ethereal. These meetings often take place in gardens filled with impossibly vibrant flowers, or in rooms bathed in soft, golden light. The deceased appear younger and healthier than in their final days, radiating peace and wisdom. These reunions frequently provide closure and healing for those still processing grief.

Historical figures encountered during astral projection tend to emerge in environments reflecting their era. Someone might meet Leonardo da Vinci in his workshop, surrounded by unfinished inventions and anatomical drawings. Others report connecting with ancient philosophers in Greek temples or meditation masters in Himalayan caves. These encounters often yield insights that feel both personally relevant and universally applicable.

The impact of these experiences typically extends well beyond the projection itself. Many report reduced fear of death after witnessing the continuation of consciousness beyond physical form. Others describe gaining profound clarity about life purpose or resolving long-standing emotional conflicts through these encounters. The visceral nature of astral projection often leaves participants with an unshakeable conviction in the reality of their experience, despite its departure from ordinary perception.

These experiences frequently catalyze significant life changes, inspiring people to pursue meaningful work, heal relationships, or explore spiritual practices more deeply. The direct experience of consciousness existing independently of the physical body often transforms fundamental beliefs about reality and human potential.

24

Navigating the Hypnagogic State

The hypnagogic state emerges in those precious moments between wakefulness and sleep, when consciousness begins to drift and reality softens around the edges. During this transitional phase, the mind experiences unique phenomena that blend the tangible world with dream-like elements.

Visual hallucinations often manifest as geometric patterns dancing behind closed eyelids - swirling fractals, pulsing lights, or kaleidoscopic shapes that morph and evolve. These patterns can transform into more complex imagery: faces emerging from abstract forms, landscapes materializing from nothing, or objects that seem to float in the darkness.

The auditory experience proves equally fascinating. Some people perceive their name being called, though no one is present. Others hear fragments of conversations, musical notes, or the sudden bang of a door that exists only in their mind. These sounds feel remarkably real despite having no external source.

Physical sensations accompany these experiences. The body may feel like it's floating, spinning, or sinking into the mattress. Some experience sudden muscle jerks or the sensation of falling, startling them back to full wakefulness. Time perception becomes fluid, with moments stretching or compressing unpredictably.

Thoughts during this state flow differently than in regular consciousness. Logic gives way to dream-like associations, where one idea morphs seamlessly into another without regard for conventional reasoning. A passing car's headlights might transform into thoughts about childhood memories of fireflies, which then blend into contemplations about the nature of light itself.

This state holds particular significance for creative individuals. Artists and inventors throughout history have deliberately extended their time in this twilight consciousness, allowing its unique perspectives to inform their work. The fluid thinking and vivid imagery can spark novel solutions to problems or inspire new artistic directions.

For those seeking to enhance dream recall or explore lucid dreaming, the hypnagogic state serves as a crucial gateway. By maintaining gentle awareness during this transition, practitioners can carry consciousness into the dream state while their body drifts into sleep.

The hypnagogic state offers a rich wellspring of creativity, but capturing its elusive insights requires specific techniques and preparation. A small notebook and pen placed within arm's reach of the bed allows for quick recording of impressions before they fade. Using a red light or dim lamp preserves night vision while writing, preventing full awakening that bright lights might trigger.

Some practitioners find success with voice recorders, speaking their observations in hushed tones as imagery unfolds. This proves especially useful when physical movement might disrupt the delicate balance between waking and sleeping states. The key lies in minimal movement and maintaining that twilight consciousness.

Mindfulness practices enhance awareness during this transition period. Starting with focused breathing helps quiet the analytical mind while maintaining gentle alertness. Rather than actively pursuing hypnagogic phenomena, allow them to arise naturally while maintaining the role of passive observer. This approach prevents the conscious mind from interrupting the process through over-eagerness.

Setting a clear intention before entering the hypnagogic state can guide the experience without forcing it. Simple phrases like "I remain aware as I drift to sleep" or "I observe my mind's images" help maintain focus without creating pressure or expectation. The goal is to cultivate a state of relaxed attention rather than rigid concentration.

Physical comfort plays a crucial role in sustaining hypnagogic awareness. The body should be completely supported, typically lying on the back with arms at the sides. This position reduces physical distractions while promoting an alert yet relaxed state. Some find success with a slightly elevated head position, which helps prevent drifting too quickly into sleep.

Regular practice develops familiarity with personal hypnagogic patterns. Some people experience primarily visual phenomena, while others might encounter more auditory or kinesthetic sensations. Understanding these individual tendencies allows for better preparation and more successful recording methods. A consistent practice schedule, even if brief, builds skill in navigating this unique state of consciousness.

The hypnagogic state has proven particularly fertile ground for creative breakthroughs throughout history. Salvador Dali famously harnessed this twilight consciousness by holding a key over a metal plate while sitting in his armchair. As he drifted off, the key would drop, creating a sound that awakened him to capture the vivid imagery dancing through his mind. This technique led to many of his most surreal masterpieces.

Thomas Edison employed a similar method using metal ball bearings to catch creative insights during brief dips into hypnagogia. The clatter of dropping spheres would rouse him just as his mind began generating novel solutions to technical problems. This practice contributed to his prolific invention output, including improvements to the light bulb and phonograph.

Mary Shelley's groundbreaking novel "Frankenstein" emerged from a waking dream during a hypnagogic state. The vivid image of a scientist kneeling beside his creation came to her in that liminal space between sleeping and waking, spawning one of literature's most enduring stories.

Modern creators can harness this state through structured practices. Setting a specific problem or creative challenge before entering hypnagogia focuses the mind's natural tendency to generate unusual connections. Keeping a voice recorder or sketchpad within reach allows for immediate documentation of insights without fully breaking the state.

The practice of "microdreaming" involves deliberately entering hypnagogia multiple times in short sessions. This technique maximizes exposure to the state's unique cognitive features while maintaining enough awareness to remember the experience. Creative professionals often schedule these sessions during their peak creative hours, treating them as brainstorming tools.

Inventors and artists frequently report that hypnagogic imagery offers novel combinations of existing elements, presenting familiar objects or ideas in unexpected arrangements. This natural remixing of mental content can bypass conventional thinking patterns, leading to innovative solutions that might not arise during normal waking consciousness.

The exploration of hypnagogia requires careful attention to both physical and mental safety. Creating an ideal environment starts with selecting a comfortable position that allows for relaxation without falling into deep sleep. A reclined chair often works better than lying flat, as it helps maintain a balance between wakefulness and drowsiness.

The room should be dimly lit - complete darkness can make it difficult to distinguish between hypnagogic imagery and actual visual input, while bright light may prevent relaxation. Temperature control plays a crucial role, as being too hot or cold can disrupt the delicate transition state. A slightly cool room, around 65-68°F (18-20°C), typically provides optimal conditions.

Setting clear time boundaries helps prevent unintended sleep episodes. Using a gentle alarm or timer set for 15-20 minutes allows for exploration while maintaining daily responsibilities. This structured approach also helps reduce anxiety about oversleeping or losing track of time.

Mental preparation involves establishing firm psychological anchors to reality. Before beginning, take note of specific details in the environment - the texture of the chair, the weight of your body, or the sound of breathing. These sensory markers serve as reference points if the experience becomes too intense or disorienting.

Some practitioners find it helpful to keep one hand slightly raised or maintain a light muscle tension. These physical "reality checks" provide immediate feedback about their state of consciousness. If the hand drops or tension releases completely, it signals a shift toward sleep rather than hypnagogia.

For those new to exploring this state, starting with short sessions during daylight hours can help build confidence and familiarity. This reduces the risk of sleep disruption and makes it easier to maintain awareness of the boundary between hypnagogic experiences and reality.

The practice benefits from consistency but should never be forced. If anxiety or discomfort arises, simply opening the eyes and taking a few deep breaths can help restore normal waking consciousness. This gentle approach ensures a safe and sustainable exploration of hypnagogic phenomena.

25

Exploring the Dreamscape

A dreamscape transcends the typical dream environment, creating an intricate tapestry of interconnected scenes and symbols that form a complete dream world. Unlike fragmented or disconnected dream sequences, a dreamscape presents itself as a fully realized environment with its own internal logic and consistent rules, even if they defy waking reality.

Within these expansive mental landscapes, the mind crafts elaborate settings that can span vast territories or compress entire universes into intimate spaces. A dreamscape might manifest as an endless ocean where islands float in the sky, or a single room that contains doorways to countless other dimensions. The physics and geography of these spaces often bend conventional rules - stairs might lead both up and down simultaneously, or a desert might seamlessly transition into an arctic tundra.

The creation of these vivid worlds stems from the brain's remarkable ability to synthesize memories, emotions, and imagination into cohesive environments. Drawing from both conscious and unconscious material, dreamscapes weave together familiar elements in unfamiliar ways. A childhood home might merge with a current workplace, or a city street might incorporate features from multiple places visited throughout life.

Dreamscapes play a crucial role in how our minds construct narratives during sleep. They provide the stage upon which dream stories unfold, offering rich contextual frameworks that support the dream's underlying themes and messages. The environment itself often becomes an active participant in the dream's storytelling, morphing and responding to the dreamer's emotional state or the dream's narrative progression.

These immersive dream environments serve as more than mere backdrops - they function as dynamic storytelling elements that can reflect psychological states, process emotions, or work through complex problems. A labyrinthine dreamscape might represent the dreamer's struggle with a difficult decision, while an endless horizon could symbolize unlimited potential or opportunity.

The unique architecture of dreamscapes often defies the constraints of physical space and time, allowing for experiences that would be impossible in waking life. This flexibility enables the mind to explore scenarios and possibilities unconstrained by reality, making dreamscapes powerful tools for creative problem-solving and emotional processing.

The ability to expand and explore dreamscapes can be developed through specific mental exercises and documentation techniques. Just as an artist sketches preliminary drawings before creating a masterpiece, dreamers can build their capacity to generate rich dream environments through conscious practice.

Visualization serves as a fundamental tool for enhancing dream worlds. Before sleep, spend time imagining detailed scenes with all five senses. Picture the texture of grass beneath bare feet, the scent of pine needles in a forest, or the echo of footsteps in an empty hallway. This mental rehearsal trains the brain to create more vivid settings during dreams.

A simple but effective visualization exercise involves choosing a familiar location and mentally adding new elements. Take a childhood home and imagine additional rooms, secret passages, or windows that open to unexpected vistas. This practice helps the mind become more flexible in creating and expanding dream environments.

Dream mapping offers a structured approach to documenting and navigating dreamscapes. Upon waking, sketch the layout of dream locations, marking significant features and transitions between areas. These maps need not follow conventional geography - they might show how a basement door opens into a mountaintop, or how a hallway loops impossibly back to itself.

Creating a dream atlas over time reveals patterns in personal dreamscapes. Some dreamers discover recurring locations that evolve across multiple dreams, while others notice how certain emotions correspond to specific types of environments. This documentation helps track the development of dream worlds and provides reference points for future dream exploration.

Consider mapping techniques that go beyond traditional floor plans. Circular diagrams can show how different dream locations connect, while color coding can represent emotional resonance or energy levels within different areas. Some find success using three-dimensional sketches to capture the unique spatial relationships of their dreamscapes.

These maps become more than mere records - they serve as tools for intentional dream navigation. By reviewing maps before sleep, dreamers can set intentions to revisit specific locations or explore uncharted areas of their dreamscapes. This practiced familiarity with dream territories often leads to increased awareness and control within dreams.

Dreamscapes often mirror our innermost psychological landscape, reflecting both conscious and unconscious aspects of our psyche. The environments we encounter while dreaming can reveal deep-seated emotions, unresolved conflicts, and hidden potential that may remain obscured during waking life.

Consider a recurring dreamscape of an endless corridor lined with locked doors. This setting might represent unexplored opportunities or aspects of oneself that feel inaccessible. The corridor's seemingly infinite nature could symbolize the vast potential for personal growth, while the locked doors might indicate self-imposed limitations or fears holding one back from full self-expression.

Water-based dreamscapes carry particular psychological significance. A calm lake might reflect inner peace, while turbulent oceans often symbolize emotional upheaval. The depth of water can represent layers of consciousness - the surface representing conscious awareness, while deeper waters suggest unconscious material rising to awareness.

From a spiritual perspective, dreamscapes can serve as sacred spaces for profound insights and transformative experiences. Ancient temples, mystical gardens, or celestial realms appearing in dreams may indicate a readiness for spiritual advancement. These environments often emerge when the dreamer is prepared to receive deeper wisdom or undergo significant personal transformation.

Exploring these dream environments mindfully can lead to breakthrough realizations. A barren desert dreamscape might initially seem threatening, but upon deeper exploration could reveal itself as a place of purification and spiritual testing. Similarly, finding oneself in an ancient library might represent access to universal wisdom or ancestral knowledge.

The appearance of certain dreamscape elements often correlates with stages of spiritual development. Ascending staircases, spiraling paths, or discovering hidden rooms can indicate progress along one's spiritual journey. These symbolic environments provide metaphorical spaces where inner work and spiritual growth can unfold naturally.

Regular interaction with meaningful dreamscapes can foster psychological integration and spiritual maturity. By paying attention to the details and emotional resonance of these environments, dreamers can gain valuable insights into their psychological makeup and spiritual path.

Recurring dreamscapes often reveal patterns in our psychological landscape. A frequent example involves finding oneself in an ever-expanding house, where new rooms continuously appear. These spaces typically represent undiscovered aspects of the dreamer's personality or untapped potential. The layout might shift and change, but the core feeling of discovery remains constant.

Natural dreamscapes carry potent symbolism. Mountains frequently appear as challenges to overcome, while dense forests represent periods of confusion or soul-searching. One common pattern shows dreamers encountering a familiar childhood home, but with mysterious new additions or altered architecture.

These modifications often reflect personal growth or unresolved family dynamics.

Urban dreamscapes manifest as complex cityscapes that defy physical laws. Skyscrapers might float upside down, or streets might loop impossibly back on themselves. These surreal environments frequently emerge during periods of major life transitions, suggesting the mind's attempt to reorganize and make sense of change.

The emotional resonance of dreamscapes provides crucial insights. A recurring beach setting might initially evoke peace, but closer examination reveals threatening undertows or looming storms, highlighting subconscious anxieties. Similarly, finding oneself in an endless maze can reflect feelings of being trapped in circular patterns in waking life.

Sacred or mystical dreamscapes often appear as ancient temples, crystalline caves, or ethereal gardens. These environments typically emerge during periods of spiritual questioning or growth. The architecture and atmosphere of these spaces often incorporate elements from multiple cultural traditions, suggesting universal spiritual themes rather than specific religious contexts.

Dreamscape exploration reveals how environments shift in response to emotional states. A peaceful meadow might transform into a barren wasteland when the dreamer confronts difficult emotions, while dark forests can open into sunlit clearings during moments of breakthrough or understanding. These transitions offer valuable insights into personal psychological processes and emotional patterns.

Through regular dreamscape navigation, patterns emerge that can guide personal growth. The repeated appearance of certain environments - whether threatening or nurturing - often points to areas requiring attention in waking life.

26

Recent Breakthroughs in Dream Science

Recent advances in neuroscience have revolutionized our understanding of dreams. Through cutting-edge brain imaging technologies like functional magnetic resonance imaging (fMRI) and magnetoencephalography (MEG), researchers can now observe the living brain during sleep with unprecedented clarity. These tools reveal intricate patterns of neural activity that illuminate how dreams form and function.

The development of high-resolution fMRI has been particularly groundbreaking. This technology tracks blood flow changes in the brain, showing which regions activate during different dream states. Studies using fMRI have identified increased activity in the visual cortex during vivid dreams, suggesting that the brain processes dream imagery similarly to waking visual experiences.

MEG technology offers complementary insights by measuring the magnetic fields produced by neural activity. This reveals the precise timing of brain responses during dreams, showing how different regions communicate and coordinate. MEG studies have documented distinct patterns of brain wave activity that correspond to specific types of dream experiences.

These imaging advances have mapped key neural circuits involved in dream generation. The pontine tegmentum, located in the brainstem, emerges as a crucial hub for initiating REM sleep and associated dreaming. Research shows this region triggers a cascade of neural events that activate the thalamus and cortex, creating the rich sensory experiences we know as dreams.

The amygdala and hippocampus also play vital roles in dream formation. Advanced imaging reveals these emotion and memory centers become highly active during REM sleep, explaining why dreams often incorporate emotional experiences and memories from waking life. The prefrontal cortex, responsible for logical thinking, shows reduced activity - accounting for the often bizarre and illogical nature of dreams.

Scientists have identified specific neural signatures that indicate when dreaming occurs. These patterns appear as distinct combinations of brain wave frequencies and activation patterns across different brain regions. This discovery allows researchers to predict with increasing accuracy when someone is likely experiencing a dream, even before they report it upon waking.

Recent genetic research has opened new frontiers in understanding how our DNA shapes our dream experiences. Studies examining twin populations reveal striking similarities in dream patterns between identical twins, suggesting a strong genetic component to how we dream.

Scientists have identified several gene variants that influence sleep architecture and dream intensity. The PER3 gene, involved in circadian rhythm regulation, appears particularly significant. Individuals with certain PER3 variations report more vivid and frequent dream recall. These genetic differences may explain why some people naturally remember their dreams more easily than others.

Research into the BDNF gene, which affects brain plasticity and memory formation, shows its variations can impact dream vividness and emotional content. Carriers of specific BDNF variants tend to experience more intense and emotionally charged dreams. This genetic influence helps explain individual differences in dream experiences that persist throughout life.

The COMT gene, which regulates dopamine levels in the brain, also plays a role in dream experiences. Variations in this gene affect how quickly dopamine is broken down, influencing both sleep quality and dream characteristics. People with slower dopamine metabolism often report more detailed and memorable dreams.

Genome-wide association studies have uncovered additional genetic markers linked to REM sleep duration and dream frequency. These findings suggest that our genetic makeup creates a foundation for how our brains process and generate dream experiences. Some individuals may be genetically predisposed to more frequent or vivid dreaming, while others naturally experience fewer or less memorable dreams.

Understanding these genetic influences helps explain why dream experiences can vary so dramatically between individuals, even within similar environments and circumstances. This research also suggests that while dream interpretation and recall can be improved through practice, there may be inherent genetic factors that influence our baseline capacity for dream experiences.

Recent scientific breakthroughs have illuminated why some individuals naturally recall dreams more vividly than others. Studies examining genetic markers reveal specific variations in memory-related genes that correlate with enhanced dream recall abilities. The FOXP2 gene, traditionally associated with speech and language development, shows promising links to dream memory formation and retention.

Research conducted at sleep laboratories has identified that individuals carrying certain variants of the BDNF gene demonstrate up to 35% better dream recall compared to those without these variants. These genetic differences affect how efficiently the brain consolidates and stores dream memories during the transition from sleep to wakefulness.

Beyond genetics, scientists have discovered that vitamin B6 supplementation can significantly improve dream recall. Clinical trials show that participants taking 240mg of B6 before bed reported more detailed and vivid dream memories compared to placebo groups. This breakthrough has led to further investigation of other potential supplements that might enhance dream retention.

Innovative pharmaceutical research has yielded promising results with compounds that target acetylcholine receptors in the brain. These receptors play a crucial role in memory formation during REM sleep. Early studies suggest that certain acetylcholine esterase inhibitors, when taken safely under medical supervision, may boost dream recall without significantly altering sleep architecture.

Environmental factors also influence dream recall ability. Recent studies using advanced EEG monitoring have shown that maintaining a consistent sleep schedule can increase dream recall by up to 40%. This finding supports the theory that stable circadian rhythms optimize the brain's ability to transfer dream content from short-term to long-term memory.

Researchers have also identified specific brain wave patterns associated with superior dream recall. Individuals who naturally produce more theta waves during the transition from REM sleep to wakefulness tend to remember their dreams more frequently. This discovery has led to experiments with non-invasive brain stimulation techniques aimed at enhancing these beneficial wave patterns.

These advancements offer hope for individuals struggling with dream recall, suggesting both genetic and environmental factors can be understood and potentially modified to improve dream memory retention.

Recent advances in mental health research have revolutionized our understanding of how dreams influence psychological well-being. Brain imaging studies reveal that during REM sleep, the amygdala and hippocampus - regions crucial for emotional processing and memory - show heightened activity. This discovery supports the theory that dreams serve as a natural mechanism for processing difficult emotions and traumatic experiences.

Clinical trials focusing on PTSD treatment have demonstrated promising results using dream-focused cognitive behavioral therapy. Patients who engage in structured dream analysis show a 40% reduction in nightmare frequency and intensity compared to traditional treatment methods alone. These findings suggest that actively working with dream content can help rewire trauma responses in the brain.

Anxiety disorders respond particularly well to dream-based interventions. Research indicates that recurring anxiety dreams often highlight specific triggers and unresolved concerns. By tracking these patterns, therapists can better identify root causes and develop targeted treatment strategies. Studies show that patients who maintain dream journals as part of their therapy experience a 30% greater reduction in anxiety symptoms compared to control groups.

The emergence of new neuroimaging techniques has revealed how emotional processing during dreams differs from waking states. During REM sleep, the prefrontal cortex - responsible for logical thinking - shows reduced activity while emotional centers become more active. This unique brain state allows for processing emotional experiences without the constraints of conscious reasoning.

Evidence supports that disrupted dream patterns often precede the onset of depression and other mood disorders. Regular dream analysis can serve as an early warning system, helping identify emotional disturbances before they manifest as clinical symptoms. Studies tracking dream content over time show that changes in dream themes often correlate with shifts in mental health status.

Research also demonstrates that dreams play a crucial role in fear extinction learning - the process by which fearful memories lose their emotional charge. During REM sleep, the brain repeatedly activates fear memories in a safe environment, gradually reducing their emotional impact. This natural process has inspired new therapeutic approaches for treating anxiety and phobias.

27

The Intersection of Technology and Dream Analysis

Artificial intelligence has emerged as a groundbreaking tool in dream research, offering new possibilities for understanding the complex patterns and symbols within our dreams. Modern AI algorithms can process thousands of dream reports simultaneously, identifying recurring themes and correlations that human researchers might miss.

Advanced machine learning systems now analyze dream journals through natural language processing, detecting emotional undertones and symbolic connections across vast datasets. These systems track patterns in dream content, helping identify how daily experiences influence dream narratives. For example, AI analysis has revealed that workplace stress commonly manifests in dreams about being unprepared or arriving late, appearing in 67% of work-related dream reports.

Neural networks trained on extensive dream databases can recognize subtle relationships between dream symbols and life events. These systems consider cultural contexts, personal histories, and emotional states to provide more nuanced interpretations than traditional dream dictionaries. The AI might notice that water symbolism varies significantly based on cultural background - appearing as cleansing in some contexts and threatening in others.

Personalized dream interpretation platforms now leverage AI to create individual dream profiles. These systems learn from user input over time, adapting their analysis to each person's unique symbolic language. The technology tracks how specific symbols evolve in meaning for individuals, offering insights into personal growth and emotional processing.

Recent developments in AI-driven dream analysis focus on identifying potential mental health indicators within dream patterns. These systems can flag concerning changes in dream content that might warrant professional attention, such as increased frequency of anxiety-related themes or sudden shifts in emotional tone.

Machine learning algorithms excel at detecting subtle correlations between dream content and external factors like sleep quality, diet, and daily activities. This data helps users understand how lifestyle choices impact their dream experiences. For instance, AI analysis has shown that exercise before bedtime increases the likelihood of movement-based dreams by 45%.

The integration of AI in dream research represents a bridge between scientific methodology and personal interpretation, offering both broad pattern recognition and individualized insight. However, these tools serve as supplements rather than replacements for human understanding of dreams, acknowledging the deeply personal nature of dream experiences.

Virtual reality technology has opened new frontiers in dream research, offering unprecedented ways to recreate and study dream environments. Modern VR systems can simulate the fluid, ever-changing nature of dreams, allowing researchers to examine how people interact with dream-like scenarios while conscious.

Advanced VR platforms now incorporate biofeedback sensors to monitor physiological responses during simulated dream experiences. These systems track heart rate, skin conductance, and eye movements, providing valuable data about emotional and physical reactions to different dream elements. Research shows participants experience similar physiological responses in VR dream simulations as they do during actual REM sleep, with heart rates increasing by 15-20% during stress-inducing scenarios.

Therapeutic applications of VR dream simulation help individuals confront recurring nightmares in a controlled environment. The technology allows gradual exposure to frightening dream elements, enabling users to develop coping strategies while fully aware. Studies indicate that regular exposure to VR-simulated nightmare scenarios reduces nightmare frequency by up to 60% in trauma survivors.

Dream researchers use VR to study common dream phenomena like flying, falling, or being chased. By recreating these experiences in virtual environments, scientists can better understand the neural pathways activated during similar dream states. The immersive nature of VR helps simulate the dissociative feeling often present in dreams, with 85% of participants reporting experiences closely matching their actual dream sensations.

VR technology also aids in studying lucid dreaming techniques. Programs designed to enhance dream awareness use virtual environments to practice reality checks and develop lucid dreaming skills. Users can experience shifting dreamscapes and practice maintaining consciousness during rapid environmental changes, similar to actual lucid dream experiences.

The integration of AI with VR dream simulation creates adaptive environments that respond to user emotions and behaviors. These systems can generate personalized dreamscapes based on individual dream journals and psychological profiles, offering tailored experiences for both research and therapeutic purposes.

Wearable technology has revolutionized how we track and understand dreams, moving beyond traditional lab-based sleep studies into the comfort of people's homes. Modern smartwatches and fitness trackers now incorporate advanced sensors that monitor sleep patterns with impressive accuracy, providing detailed data about REM cycles and potential dream states.

These devices track key physiological markers including heart rate variability, body temperature, and movement patterns throughout the night. The latest models can detect micro-movements of 0.1mm, allowing them to identify the rapid eye movements characteristic of REM sleep. This precise monitoring helps users identify their optimal dream recall windows based on their personal sleep architecture.

Sleep tracking apps paired with wearables now generate comprehensive sleep reports, showing exactly when users enter and exit REM sleep. This data helps identify patterns in dream frequency and duration, with most adults experiencing 4-6 REM periods per night lasting 10-60 minutes each. Users can correlate this information with their dream journal entries to better understand their personal dream patterns.

The real-time monitoring capabilities of wearable devices reveal how the body responds during different types of dreams. Heart rate typically increases by 5-15 beats per minute during emotionally charged dreams, while skin temperature fluctuations can indicate stress responses during nightmares. This physiological data provides objective measures to complement subjective dream reports.

Advanced sleep tracking devices now incorporate smart alarm features that gently wake users during optimal points in their sleep cycle, typically at the end of a REM period. This strategic timing has shown to improve dream recall by up to 40% compared to arbitrary wake times. Users report clearer, more detailed dream memories when awakened during these carefully calculated windows.

The aggregated data from millions of wearable users has created unprecedented insights into population-level sleep and dream patterns. This massive dataset reveals how factors like age, season, and daily activities influence dream frequency and intensity, helping researchers identify universal patterns in human dreaming experience.

The rapid advancement of dream-tracking technology raises important ethical questions about privacy and data security. Personal dream experiences, captured through wearables and apps, contain intimate details about an individual's subconscious mind, fears, desires, and emotional state. This sensitive information requires careful protection to prevent misuse or exploitation.

Many sleep tracking companies now collect vast amounts of dream-related data, including physiological responses, sleep patterns, and user-reported dream content. While this data proves valuable for research, questions arise about ownership rights and consent. Users often agree to terms of service without fully understanding how their intimate dream experiences might be analyzed, shared, or monetized.

The commercialization of dream data presents particular concerns. Companies may use aggregated dream patterns to develop targeted advertising or predict consumer behavior. Some firms already analyze dream content to recommend products based on emotional states or subconscious desires. This practice raises debates about manipulation and the boundaries between personal privacy and commercial interests.

Ethical guidelines for dream research technology emphasize several key principles. First, informed consent must clearly explain how dream data will be collected, stored, and used. Second, individuals should maintain control over their personal dream information, with options to delete or restrict access. Third, anonymization protocols must protect user identity when dream data is used for research or commercial purposes.

The potential for dream surveillance through technology also raises alarm. Advanced wearables that record physiological responses during dreams could reveal mental health conditions, trauma, or personal secrets. Without proper safeguards, this information could be vulnerable to hackers, employers, or insurance companies seeking to make discriminatory decisions.

Researchers and developers must balance scientific progress with ethical considerations. This includes implementing robust security measures, establishing clear boundaries for data usage, and respecting individual privacy rights. Regular audits and transparency reports can help ensure compliance with ethical guidelines while maintaining public trust in dream research technology.

The field requires ongoing dialogue between technology developers, researchers, ethicists, and users to establish comprehensive standards for responsible innovation in dream tracking and analysis. These discussions must address both current capabilities and potential future developments in dream monitoring technology.

28

Conclusion

Throughout this exploration of dreams, we've journeyed through multiple dimensions of understanding - from the intricate mechanics of REM sleep to the rich tapestry of cultural interpretations spanning centuries and continents. The scientific foundations we've examined reveal dreams as essential functions of our brain's processing, memory consolidation, and emotional regulation systems. Modern neuroscience has illuminated how different brain waves and neural networks contribute to our dream experiences, while sleep studies have mapped the precise stages where our most vivid dreams emerge.

We've delved into the symbolic language of dreams, discovering how our subconscious mind communicates through archetypes, metaphors, and personal symbols. These symbols, whether universal or deeply personal, serve as bridges between our conscious and unconscious minds. The analytical tools provided - from dream journaling techniques to mindfulness practices - offer practical methods for decoding these messages.

Our journey has embraced diverse cultural perspectives, acknowledging how different societies throughout history have valued and interpreted dreams. From indigenous dream practices to Eastern philosophical approaches and Western psychological frameworks, each tradition contributes valuable insights into the human experience of dreaming.

The practical tools shared throughout these chapters empower readers to develop their own relationship with dreams. Simple yet effective techniques like maintaining optimal sleep conditions, practicing mindful awareness, and recording dreams immediately upon waking create a foundation for deeper dream work. The integration of scientific understanding with personal insight allows for a balanced approach to dream interpretation.

We've explored how dreams serve as catalysts for personal growth, emotional healing, and creative inspiration. The examination of dream symbolism, combined with techniques for lucid dreaming and nightmare transformation, provides pathways for psychological development and emotional resilience. Modern technology's role in dream research offers exciting possibilities while raising important ethical considerations about privacy and data protection.

These varied approaches to understanding dreams - scientific, spiritual, cultural, symbolic, and practical - come together to form a comprehensive framework for working with dreams in daily life. This integration allows readers to draw from multiple perspectives while developing their own authentic approach to dream exploration.

The field of dream research continues to evolve rapidly, with new technologies offering unprecedented insights into the sleeping brain. Brain imaging techniques become more sophisticated each year, allowing researchers to map dream activity with increasing precision. Artificial intelligence and machine learning now help analyze vast databases of dream reports, revealing patterns that were previously hidden.

Wearable devices track sleep patterns and brain waves with growing accuracy, making it possible to better understand personal dream cycles. Virtual reality applications are being developed to recreate and study dream environments, potentially offering new ways to work with recurring dreams or nightmares. These technological advances may soon provide tools for enhancing dream recall and lucidity.

Neuroscientists are uncovering new connections between dreams and mental health, suggesting additional therapeutic applications. Research into memory consolidation during sleep reveals how dreams might be used more effectively for learning and skill development. Studies of consciousness and altered states continue to shed light on the nature of dream experiences.

The intersection of Eastern and Western approaches to dreams remains a rich area for exploration. Traditional practices like meditation and mindfulness are being integrated with scientific understanding, creating more comprehensive approaches to dream work. Cultural perspectives on dreams continue to offer valuable insights that complement scientific findings.

Stay curious about your own dream experiences. Each dream journal entry, each moment of reflection, adds to your personal understanding. Consider joining dream study groups or participating in dream research projects. Online communities offer opportunities to share experiences and learn from others while maintaining privacy.

Remember that dream exploration is a lifelong journey. As science advances our understanding of dreams, new tools and techniques will emerge. Remain open to these developments while trusting your intuition and personal experience. Your dreams will continue to offer insights and guidance as you grow and change.

The future of dream research holds exciting possibilities for understanding consciousness, healing trauma, and enhancing creativity. By staying engaged with this evolving field, you can incorporate new findings into your personal practice while contributing to our collective understanding of dreams.

As you continue your journey with dreams, maintain curiosity and openness. Each dream, whether vivid or fragmentary, carries potential for insight. Even seemingly mundane dreams can reveal profound truths when approached with patience and awareness.

Dreams speak in the language of possibility. They remind us that our minds contain vast unexplored territories waiting to be discovered. In understanding our dreams, we better understand ourselves and our place in the larger tapestry of human experience.

Remember: Dreams are not just stories we tell ourselves in the dark. They are opportunities for growth, healing, and transformation. They connect us to our deepest selves and to the collective wisdom of humanity. Trust in their guidance, respect their mystery, and remain open to the insights they offer.

Your journey with dreams is uniquely yours. May you continue to explore, discover, and grow through the extraordinary landscape of your dreaming mind.

.

Shine a Light on the Power of Dreams

"The meaning of life is to find your gift. The purpose of life is to give it away." –
Pablo Picasso

Dreams are like secret messages from your mind, waiting to be decoded. They speak in symbols, weaving stories from your thoughts, fears, and joys. Imagine helping someone unlock those messages—someone who's curious about their dreams but doesn't know where to start.

That's where you come in.

My mission with *Dream Interpretation Decoded* is to make understanding dreams easier and more personal for everyone. Dreams aren't just random pictures or feelings—they're your mind's way of communicating in its own special language.

But to reach more people, I need your help.

Most people decide what book to pick up based on reviews. By leaving a review, you're helping someone else take the first step in understanding their dreams.

Your review could help...

- Someone understand we each have a unique dream dictionary to the meaning behind signs and symbols in our dreams.

- Another find peace in know that science and spirituality complement each other in understanding dreams.

- A friend discover the joy of connecting with their subconscious mind.

- One more dreamer find the tools they need to make sense of their inner world.

It doesn't cost anything and takes just a minute, but your review could make a big difference in someone's journey to understanding their dreams.

To leave a review, just scan the QR code below:

If you've enjoyed *Dream Interpretation Decoded* and love helping others, thank you from the bottom of my heart. Together, we can inspire more people to explore the fascinating world of dreams.

Victor Nyx